RIDER'S DIGEST: Showing and Combined Training

SANDRA KAUFFMAN

arco
New York, New York

Published by Arco Publishing Company, Inc.
219 Park Avenue South, New York, N.Y. 10003

Library of Congress Cataloging in Publication Data

Main entry under title:

Rider's digest.

1. Horse-shows—Addresses, essays, lectures.
2. Horses—Showing—Addresses, essays, lectures.
3. Show riding—Addresses, essays, lectures. 4. Three-day event (Horsemanship)—Addresses, essays, lectures.
I. Kauffman, Sandra.

SF295.R52 798′.23 76-28792
ISBN 0-668-04115-3 (Cloth Edition)

Printed in the United States of America

For

My Mother

Acknowledgments

Credit for the contents of *Rider's Digest* belongs to the authors whose articles appear on the following pages and whose professionalism is manifest not only in their writing but also in the generosity with which they share their work and talent. Many editors also found the time to secure articles, photographs, and information for this book despite heavy work schedules and deadline pressures of their own. For help and consideration so graciously given, many thanks go to E. Hartley Edwards of *Riding* Magazine, Carolyn Banks of *Horse Play*, Snowden Carter of the Maryland Horse Breeders Association, Dick Spenser III of *Western Horseman*, Tex Rogers of *Horseman*, Jack Lewis of *Horse and Horseman*, Ray Rich of *Horse & Rider*, C. L. Pettit of *The Utah Equestrian*, and most especially to Marie Lafrenz of *American Horseman*, Fifi Coles of *USCTA News*, and Pamela Goold of *Practical Horseman*. I am particularly grateful to Sheila Wall Hundt, Paul Nigro, and Maxine Solat for many kindnesses; to the staff of H. Kauffman & Sons Saddlery Company for their technical assistance; and to my husband, whose patience, humor, and tact were an unfailing source of encouragement.

Contents

SECTION III—COMBINED TRAINING AND THE THREE-DAY EVENT

Introduction

If magazines had existed in the Garden of Eden, it is unlikely that Eve would have tasted the apple. A food editor would have outlined the hazards of eating uncooked fruit, a beauty editor would have said that peaches were better for the skin, and an astrology chart would have advised newly created ladies against friendships with serpents. Armed with so much good advice, Eve certainly would have improved her performance as First Lady.

Teaching people how to improve in virtually everything they undertake has become the specialty of today's magazines. A major source of information and instruction, their range is truly remarkable. Whatever your interest (be it pedestrian, arcane or even obsolete), someone somewhere is publishing a magazine for you. Whenever a new idea takes hold, whenever a new trend starts, a new magazine is sure to follow.

Today, our national concern with physical fitness has led to a dramatic increase in the number of magazines dealing with sports and outdoor life. The riding magazine is a perfect case in point. A recent trade journal listed one hundred and eighteen publications devoted exclusively to the care and training of horses! The field is so wide that every breed and every type of riding has its own magazine and every magazine has its own style and form. The quality of the material is uncommonly high. The articles are written by experts, each focusing on a special area of interest and each imparting something of value—a hint, an observation, a viewpoint, or a technique.

By arranging these fine pieces in topical book form, *Rider's Digest* hopes to give them a life beyond the transience of the periodical and make them permanently available to horsemen. And, just as horsemen breed "the best to the best," we have tried to choose the "best" articles available and join them together by subject to produce an anthology of unbeatable bloodline.

SECTION I

THE HORSE SHOW

LEARNING THE RULES

Bad Form and All That—

The American Horse Show Classes

By
ROBIN SERFASS

One of the best articles on horse shows in America was written by an American —for an English audience. Originally published in a special Show issue of Riding *Magazine, this is its first appearance in this country.*

Reprinted by permission of *Riding* Magazine. Subscriptions: Tower House, Southampton Street, London WC2E, England. 4.60LS United Kingdom; 5.50LS overseas (12 issues).

Horse shows in the United States reflect the wide variety of riding styles and different breeds of horses that have, out of necessity, developed over the years, America being such a vast country with such varied regions. Shows in all areas had to cater to these differences, thus the typical horse show in the United States offers a broad spectrum of classes for various styles of riding and breeds of horses.

Riding styles can be classified into three distinct types; *hunt seat,* which originated in England for foxhunting, *stock seat,* used by the American cowboy for herding and roping cattle, and finally *saddle seat,* which developed in the Old South when plantations and huge estates were the order of the day.

The various breeds and types of horses include the following: Appaloosa, Arabian, Morgan, Quarter Horse, Palomino, Pinto, Paint, Pony of the Americas, Welsh Pony, Shetland Pony, Hackney Pony, American Saddlebred, Tennessee Walking Horse and Thoroughbred. Although all breeds can be shown in any of the three seats, usually one seat is predominant. For example, American Saddlebred and Tennessee Walking Horses are usually ridden in saddle seat classes, while the Quarter Horse is most commonly seen in stock seat classes and Thoroughbreds are used primarily in hunter and jumper events. Breed shows offer both halter (in hand) and performance classes, with the native costume class being one of the most popular and colorful performance events. All the various breeds have their own associations, which determine the regulations and rules for that breed and for the breed shows.

Most general shows in the United States are recognized and ruled by the American Horse Shows Association, the governing body of horse shows across America. The A.H.S.A. works in conjunction with the various breed organizations. A typical horse show of one to 12 days would offer classes for hunters, jumpers, stock horses, trail horses, pleasure horses, walking horses, three- and five-gaited horses, harness horses, roadsters, and harness and Hackney ponies. Most shows are divided into three sessions, morning, afternoon and evening, with a class of each type in each session. In a typical show, classes can generally be broken down into the various riding styles or 'seats.'

The hunt seat style of riding includes hunter, jumper and equitation, or horsemanship, classes. Hunter competitions in the United States are quite different from those found in Britain, as all American show hunters perform over fences and are judged on their style of jumping the fences and their pace between the jumps. There is only one event, the hunter under saddle class, in which a hunter is judged exclusively on his walk, trot, canter, and gallop. The judge, or judges, *never* rides the hunter in American horse shows, as the emphasis is on the horse's performance over jumps and the judge's evaluation is visual only. In the A.H.S.A. rule book, the rules for the hunter division state that, "Judges shall penalize unsafe jumping and *BAD FORM* over fences, whether the fence was touched or untouched." Hunters are then subdivided into a wide variety of divisions, which include *green* hunter, for horses in their first or second year of showing, pony hunters for animals under 14.2 h.h., junior hunters, to be shown by a rider under 18 years of age, adult/amateur hunters, ridden by non-professional exhibitors over 18 years old, working hunters, in which the horse's conformation is never considered, and, finally, conformation hunters, in which the horse's conformation counts for 25 to 50 percent of the marks awarded in the class. Green, junior, pony, and amateur hunters jump a course of fences 3 ft. 6 in. to 3 ft. 9 in. in height while working and conformation hunters are required to jump 4 ft. to 4 ft. 6 in. The emphasis in judging in all divisions is on the way the horse approaches and jumps his fences. A good hunter should 'flow' around a course, taking off and landing over the fences without any perceptible alteration of his stride.

Jumper events in the States closely resemble those found in Britain, but again more variety is offered within the jumper division. Classes are held for preliminary jumpers, or horses who have not won $1,500.00 in the jumper division; intermediate jumpers, who have won between $1,500.00 and $3,000.00; open jumpers who have won over $3,000.00; junior jumpers, to be ridden by a junior exhibitor under 18; and amateur/owner jumpers, in which a horse must be shown by his non-professional owner who is over 18 years old. Preliminary and intermediate classes are designed for the green and novice horse, but these horses can compete in the open jumper divisions, as can junior and amateur/owner jumpers. However, open jumpers are not allowed to compete in either the preliminary or intermediate divisions, but are eligible for junior or amateur/owner classes with a qualified rider.

Equitation classes are judged strictly on the rider's performance and style, either on the flat or over a course of fences. The horse's style of jumping is not considered, as only the rider is being judged, and equitation events are limited to junior riders. This division is always the largest at any show, often with over 100 riders in a single class. The second style of riding is saddle seat, which also includes equitation classes for junior riders. Most horses shown in the saddle seat division are American Saddlebreds, a breed of large, high-headed horses with natural animation. Saddlebreds are shown under saddle in three-gaited events, where the animal has a shaved mane and tail and performs at a walk, trot and canter; in five-gaited classes, where the horse wears a full, flowing mane and tail and performs, in addition to the three gaits, at the two artificial gaits, the slow gait and the rack; and in fine harness events, again performing with a full mane and tail, at an animated walk and a show trot. Horses in Saddlebred classes are judged on their brilliance, animation, quality and conformation. One exhibitor observed that, "You want a horse who looks as though he is going to explode, but doesn't."

In the equitation division, junior riders are judged on their horsemanship at the three gaits only, as a five-gaited horse is too animated and shows at greater speed than a three-gaited mount. Again, the rider's style, poise, and performance are the criteria for judging.

Tennessee Walking Horses are shown in the saddle-seat style of riding at three gaits, the flat-footed walk, the running walk, and the canter. The spectacular running walk was developed on the plantations of the Old South when an owner required a comfortable yet speedy-gaited horse to oversee his property. It is a gait unique to the Tennessee Walking Horse and most of the judging in this division is on the speed and action a horse shows in the running walk.

Ponies are catered for in the saddle seat division with three- and five-gaited classes and ponies compete in roadster and pleasure driving events. Several breeds of ponies can be found showing in a typical American horse show. The Hackney pony is a recognized breed and is shown in harness with a short mane and tail while a harness pony can be of any breed and is shown with a long mane and tail. Both Hackney and harness ponies are shown pulling a four-wheeled vehicle called a 'viceroy' at a slow trot and an animated show trot. Classes for roadster ponies, as in those for roadster horses, are also open to any breed unless otherwise specified. Drivers wear racing silks while sitting in a two-wheeled racing-type buggy and roadsters perform at a trot in both directions of the ring, and at a trot at speed only on the right rein. The emphasis in roadster classes is on speed as well as brilliance and animation, while in harness and Hackney pony events, the emphasis in judging is placed on the pony's style rather than his speed.

The third style of riding in the United States is stock seat or Western riding. Stock seat riders use a Western saddle which has a horn on the pommel, originally (and still) used for roping cattle, a high cantle for comfort, and full skirts for protection. Within the stock seat division a wide variety of classes is offered. As in hunt seat and saddle seat, equitation events are filled with junior riders being judged strictly on their style. Stock seat equitation can be on the flat, in which riders show only at the walk, jog (slow trot), and lope (slow canter), or on a stock routine where horse and rider perform a full stock routine complete with fast, full turns on the hocks, a figure eight with flying changes at the lope, and a sliding stop in which the horse is stopped instantly from a gallop and slides 20 to 40 ft. on his hind feet. Stock horses are required to perform this routine in their classes too, but only the horse is judged with no consideration given to the rider's form or style. In addition to the described 'dry work' stock routine, stock horses are often asked to work a cow in order to demonstrate their quickness, speed, agility, and, most important, their 'cow sense.' Although Western classes at most general shows are open to horses of any breed over 14.1 h.h., Quarter Horses are by far the most widely used in this division.

Other Western classes include those for trail horses, in which a horse must negotiate a certain number of obstacles that might be found while riding out on the trail. These obstacles usually include a gate which must be opened and closed while mounted; a pattern which the horse must back or side-pass through; step-overs which the horse must walk or trot over without touching; a bridge for the horse to carefully walk over; a small fence to jump and a pond to step through. Trail horses are judged on their willingness and caution over and through the obstacles, and they are then judged on the rail at the walk, jog and lope.

Pleasure classes are most popular in Western riding, but are also found in the hunt and saddle seat divisions. Pleasure classes in all three seats emphasize manners, performance, conformation and the suitability of horse to rider. In Western pleasure classes, conformation and appearance are especially important, so most horses are beautifully groomed and appointed. In all three seats, horses show at only three gaits: in Western, at a walk, jog, and lope; in hunt and saddle seat, at the walk, trot and canter; and, in all cases, horses are expected to be well behaved and an enjoyable ride. The pleasure class is found in every show, breed or general, as it is the least specialized and least demanding class. Many green horses and riders begin their show ring careers in pleasure classes.

Most horses found competing in American horse shows, regardless of division, are under the direction of a professional horse trainer. These men and women operate public or private stables where they train horses and riders for show ring competition. A trainer will usually specialize in one of the three seats, and often he will specialize even further within his division. For example, a trainer will sometimes handle junior hunters and jumpers and equitation horses only, acting primarily as an instructor, while another trainer will concentrate on developing open jumpers, without teaching any riders or showing hunters. In any case, a trainer is usually responsible for a number of horses under his personal supervision both at home and 'on the road' at shows.

There can be no doubt that the typical horse show in the United States has something to offer for everyone. Exhibitors and spectators alike can be entertained by the colorful, exciting, and often unique classes found at American shows.

The Horse Show Steward

By
DIANE L. MORGAN

The Horse Show Steward is seldom seen or heard from in the ring. However, his role is of vital importance to every exhibitor and this much-needed article explains why.

What is the role of the horse show steward? What does the steward do for the exhibitor, for the judge, and for horse show management? For in order to do his (or her) job fully, he must serve all three.

The steward is the official representative of the association under whose affiliation the horse show is being held. If the show is a member show of the American Horse Shows Association, the steward serves as this official body's "spokesman." He is responsible for the correct conduct of the show (within the limits of the rules of the association), and he can assist in the interpretation of questions arising in regard to the rules. Frequently he will be called upon for aid above and beyond this specific category.

What can the steward do for the exhibitor? He can assist on problems of proper attire, of what is expected in the class specifications, and of whether an entry is eligible in a particular event. If an exhibitor wishes to speak to a judge, he must first request of a steward (or show management) the right to do so. Then a proper time for this meeting will be arranged.

If an exhibitor wishes to file a protest (if there has been a violation of the rules), the steward should assist in order to make certain that the alleged protest can be substantiated by personal testimony at a hearing or by sworn statements, and that the evidence and witnesses are properly recorded.

It must be remembered that the steward has no authority in connection with either the management of the show or the judging of the show. Stewards must observe, investigate, and report any violation to the show committee, and make recommendations for improving the show where necessary. He shall report any violations to the governing association in his report following the show, along with any charge he has made. And where specific rules do not apply, the intent of the rules must serve as a guideline.

The steward referred to here is not to be confused with the ring "steward" or ringmaster —the one who stands in the ring assisting the judge during classes. The official horse show steward is almost never in the show ring unless called upon by the judge to answer some problem. When the show is a member of the American Horse Shows Association, the official steward cannot act in any capacity which is not directly involved with the function of his duties. For example, he cannot serve as ringmaster, announcer, clerk, secretary, manager, etc. The steward is there in an advisory capacity only, and has no authority in the management or judging of the show. Many regional horse show associations have provided for stewards, with their responsibilities based upon the AHSA rules for stewards. What the AHSA steward can do to aid the exhibitor is the subject of this article.

Nothing can help to clarify a particular situation better than an example. Suppose you enter a horse show and find, according to the time schedule, that your class will be the first event in Ring B at 1 p.m. Then an announcement is made at noon that your class has been moved to Ring C at 1 p.m. And you have been to Ring C and found it is very dusty and only partly enclosed by a small, loose rope. What do you do? You call for the steward. It is just possible that the steward has already gone to the show management and requested something be done about Ring C, but management claims they've had no complaints.

The steward can only suggest, or at most, charge show management, which could result in censure or a monetary fine at a later date, but would not help the ring conditions at present. So now you come along with a complaint. And you have just possibly provided the steward with his necessary ammunition to get Ring C fixed up.

There is always the possibility that as an exhibitor you have a complaint that the steward could not possibly be aware of. So don't keep it a secret, tell the steward. If it's a management problem, you can go directly to the show management, but very often it is difficult to find just the right person for the trouble spot. But here the steward should be able to guide you on the correct course.

If a rule violation in the ring has occurred, you should report it immediately to the steward (after all, he's bound to miss a few problems); as a good exhibitor, it is your responsibility to do so. Of course, even here it may well be possible that the steward cannot always correct the situation at once—he may only be able to work out a compromise which is not always acceptable to everyone.

Example: a class that was divided in two sections has an incorrect number called back for the final ride, and it is undetected until following the final placing of the class. Then in checking the figures, the correct number is found, and this exhibitor wishes some form of restitution.

The class cannot be rejudged, and the mistake can be a costly one. Sometimes management will refund an entry fee or permit an additional entry in another class; this is seldom satisfactory in any case. Here was an error that was not detected in time to correct, so a steward can only mediate in this particular situation.

If you, as an exhibitor, have a question on measurement (height of pony, length of hoof) see the steward. When the show management has a time set up for measurement, be there promptly with the animal in question. If you find you cannot be there, make special arrangements with the steward to personally assist you. If shows are spot-checking length of hoofs and you think you might have a long-toed entry, get a measurement ahead of time so you can plan for reshoeing if needed.

Some shows are laid out in a large area and require extensive public address systems. Some are quite adequate, but let's face it, some aren't! If you can't hear class calls, let the steward know about it. But keep in mind, the steward may *not* be able to get that speaker fixed in your barn, so keep an eye out yourself for how fast the classes are proceeding in the ring. Remember, you are responsible for getting to the ring on time—and those barn calls are just a courtesy. Also keep in mind that electronic failure plus human failure can be a deadly combination that might cause you to miss your event, so stay posted *all the time!*

Perhaps you are a new exhibitor—and new to the American Horse Shows Association drug testing program. After winning a class (or maybe placing second or third) one day, you may be met by the steward with a form that you are to sign. Be prepared. This is a simple notification that you have accepted the fact that your horse is to be tested for drugs. You must sign this notification (or get your trainer or the horse's owner to sign), or you are in violation of the rules. Stewards are willing to explain the program to you, but try to be informed and save time for everyone. Learn about the drug testing program in advance or discuss it with the steward when there is ample time to permit it.

Should you decide to be in an amateur event at an AHSA show, you must possess a current AHSA amateur card. Horse show secretaries can provide you with the proper forms. But if you have questions regarding the rules or the form, see the steward. Who knows? You may not be an amateur according to the rules. So check into it before you sign up. And remember, an owners-to-ride class requires that you be an amateur-owner, unless specific local rules have stated otherwise.

When exhibiting in a new division, don't assume that all the rules in your former division will necessarily apply. While junior exhibitors can show stallions (if so stated in the prize list) in some divisions, they cannot show stallions in the Saddlebred junior exhibitor divisions. Be sure to check with the steward on division rules when you are on unfamiliar territory.

Exhibitors must keep in mind that a steward cannot be a "policeman." He suggests, he instructs, he recommends, but he does not arrest, impede, or obstruct any part of the show. Remember, his only artillery is the official charge against the violator, be he judge, manager, or exhibitor. And charges, just as protests, take time and follow certain procedures.

When you approach a steward for aid or instruction, be prepared with proper questions, substantial facts, and necessary proof. But whatever your need, don't forget the steward—he's there to serve you, too!

PREPARING FOR THE EVENT

Preparing a horse for the show ring takes many months of dedicated effort. His training, of course, is all-important, but without proper care and nutrition as well, he cannot hope to compete successfully. In the articles that follow, champion rider Ann Davis Williams helps you to plan a winning program; E. Hartley Edwards, editor of *Riding* Magazine, tells you how to get your horse in blue-ribbon condition; and show expert Gina M. Staton lets you in on the secrets of the professional groom.

Preparing for the Horse Show

By
ANN DAVIS WILLIAMS

You can spot a professional in a horse show. He's relaxed, happy, and having a good time. An amateur is more likely to be stiff and nervous. Shows are not supposed to be frightening, but until a rider has some show experience and some success he will miss a lot of fun and excitement.

Careful planning and preparation are important to be successful in the show ring. By observing various showing techniques, the amateur equestrian can look just as good and sometimes even better than professionals. A few hints on training methods, conditioning, and grooming will often produce a winning horse and rider team.

A good show horse starts with proper care and feeding. No matter how beautiful the color or conformation of a horse, if he is not in good condition he can never successfully compete in a show. If you expect to have a chance to place in any event, your horse must be in *top* show condition. This means that the horse must be neither too fat (showing lack of work) nor too thin.

Besides being fed properly, the horse should be worked regularly. One trainer suggests that a horse be ridden every other day so he will keep interested in his work and not become ring-sour. After a reasonable work period, stop riding if the horse is working well. A horse is a creature of habit and will soon learn that if he performs correctly he will be rewarded. There are many other ways to exercise a horse besides ring work. Lounging and "walkers" are excellent methods of exercise.

There is no completely "right" or "wrong" way to work a horse. The method that works best for *you* will produce the best results.

Carefully consider the type of class in which to enter your horse. Both the rider and the horse can become frustrated unless the proper selection is made. This selection depends on both the qualities and shortcomings of the individual horse and rider. Not many horses can look good several different ways, although it is possible if you choose your horse carefully. If this route is chosen, take the events separately until the horse knows what he is doing. Some horses won't take two events at once, and this is also difficult for an inexperienced rider.

If an English horse looks the part—he has an edge before he starts. This is true of the rider also. Many English exhibitors seen in an English pleasure class seem to be overworking, look rigid or artificial, and don't blend with their horses. The rider must always present a smooth and attractive picture.

Judges usually want a Western horse working easy, so that it looks like the rider really isn't doing anything. Never override. You don't want to look as if you have to over-cue a horse to make him work properly. Relaxation is especially important in a Western pleasure class, but it is necessary to be easy and relaxed in any pleasure event.

Grooming is important in order to present the best possible appearance of the horse and rider to the judge and spectators. Some exhibitors will win a class on the same horse an amateur can't because they know how good grooming catches the judge's eye.

There are many different types of equipment and grooming products available today. Grooming methods differ from person to person, but usually it takes two or three kinds of brushes, a good set of clippers, soap and water, and a lot of hard work. Clean dress and tack are essential, for this will certainly be observed in the show ring.

Try to get your horse to the showgrounds in plenty of time before the show. Many exhibitors have found that it is sometimes beneficial to get the horse into the show ring before their class. This gives the horse the opportunity to look around at his strange surroundings, to know what you will expect of him there. Sometimes the mistake is made of working the horse down directly before the show. A tired horse is not a pretty horse. You can see the difference in performance between a horse that has been ridden for hours before the class and a horse that is ready and willing to perform in the ring. The horse that is well-rested, but *relaxed*, is alert, proud, and brilliant in his performance. He is not "sour" and is willing to work for his handler.

The key to a successful performance is *relaxation.* One way to relax your horse before entering the ring is to "camp" or "live" on the horse. Walk your horse around the arena and let him look around. Go through his gaits two or three times around the ring, and then stop, talk to friends, and relax. This way the horse does not become frightened or upset, and it gives the rider a chance to relax, also.

Some exhibitors will close a horse up in a stall or trailer just before a class. This makes the horse alert and high-spirited when he is brought out of his enclosure and taken into the ring. This procedure, of course, depends on the individual horse, handler, and class. A "high" horse may become unruly and difficult to handle unless he is relaxed and given a chance to get used to his surroundings.

Don't get discouraged. Ring experience is necessary for everyone; even the best of trainers had to start somewhere. Just remember to always look and perform as perfectly as possible. Then even if you don't place, you will know you have given a good performance—which is what showing is all about!

The competition is growing larger and getting better all the time. In order to be successful, your horse must be in top condition, well-exercised, completely trained, and expertly groomed. This means a lot of attention to detail and hard work, but it *can* be rewarding.

Fit to Show

By
E. HARTLEY EDWARDS

Reprinted by permission of *Riding* Magazine. Subscriptions: Tower House, Southampton Street, London WC2E, England. 4.60LS United Kingdom, 5.50LS overseas (12 issues).

Conditioning a horse or pony involves bringing the animal to the peak of physical fitness necessary for the particular activity for which he is intended. There are, of course, numerous activities in which horses are engaged, and what is a suitable condition for one pursuit may be quite the reverse for another. The conditioning of a racehorse, for instance, is far different from that of a hunter or a show horse. It is the latter with which this article is concerned.

The objective, in this instance, is to present a horse who, while being fit enough to carry out the work required of him in the ring, carries sufficient flesh to show off his conformation to best advantage, and to accentuate any 'presence' that he may possess.

The problem, insofar as the physical condition is concerned, is to strike the happy medium. Few exhibitors would show a horse in anything approaching racing condition, lean, hard-muscled and carrying not one superfluous ounce, but not a few tend towards showing their horses over-fat. Some may do so deliberately, thinking to disguise conformational defects, although, in fact, few judges will be deceived by the ploy. Others, genuinely enough, believe show condition to relate to a plump rotundity. The disadvantages to showing a horse fat are numerous and should be obvious to all. A fat horse can give the impression of being 'overtopped,' his body appearing to be too big for his legs to support; he will certainly not be able to gallop effectively and it is very likely that he will be listless and that his action will be restricted in his other paces. This is particularly true of ponies.

The condition to be aimed for is one in which the horse appears big, but not too much so; is nicely rounded, but not so well covered that there is not a clear definition of the well-developed muscle formation. He needs to look the picture of health, with a bloom on his coat, a clear, alert eye and be sufficiently gay and interested in the proceedings to give a lively, responsive ride to a competent horseman without becoming ill-disciplined.

It would be nice if, at this point, it was possible to lay down exactly the types of food and quantities, the sort of exercise and its duration, the time spent on grooming and strapping, etc., that would produce this condition. Unfortunately, that will never be so. The conditioning program will vary according to each individual horse and will vary again between horse and pony and yet again between ridden and in-hand classes.

There are, however, requirements that will be common to all show exhibits. Clearly, good feeding, using the best quality ingredients, is a necessity for any animal, as are regular exercise, grooming and strapping. But it is as well to remember that physical appearance is only a half of conditioning. Of equal importance is the horse's mental state.

In the preparation of the show horse the first and obvious essential is that he should be wormed—he cannot be conditioned until his insides are in good order. Thereafter, possibly the most important factor is the provision of the best hay that can be obtained. Today, this may present a difficulty but without good hay the rest of the food will not be put to its best use.

Horses that need building up can be fed a ration of around 2 lb. boiled barley per day in addition to hay and oats. Most horses also appreciate dried calf milk which is a wonderful fattener. Poor feeders can be tempted by adding molasses, carrots and apples to the feeds and varying the contents of each one. Boiled linseed can be fed once a week, and twice in the week when the new summer coats are coming through, to give an extra 'bloom.' Since show horses are stabled during the summer, freshly cut grass should be included in the diet and it is no bad thing to allow them an hour or so at grass during the day; it is a very good way of preventing boredom. Bran, once part of the staple diet, is now, in some areas, so much like sawdust as to be useless and so expensive as to be prohibitive. Its laxative effect can, however, be replaced by giving a handful of Epsom salts in water once a week. Freshly cut dandelions and even nettles are excellent blood coolers, and dandelions have long been held to keep a bloom on the coat.

Ponies are more likely to be over-fat than too thin and the only solution is long, slow exercise and a drastic reduction of the bulk hay intake. Rolls of fat on either side of the withers can be reduced in part by exercising with a rug under a cellophane sheet laid over the offending parts. This will cause the pony to sweat freely but one has to be careful not to cause blistering. Fat ponies also lose their waistlines, making saddle fitting a difficulty. Exercise in a girth covered with a piece of rubber tubing will assist the formation of a waist and it will also help if the pony wears a body roller in the stable.

On the principle of 'no oats, no ambition' most show ponies will need to be fed corn. The trouble here is that when the pony has sufficient corn to show himself off he may be too much for his rider. In such cases, nuts plus 1 lb. of bruised barley a day may be a more acceptable substitute.

Summer coats should be through for the early shows but much work is often necessary to get rid of the old winter coat. If the horse has been clipped, much hand rubbing will improve the coat, otherwise use must be made of a rubber curry comb. To encourage the new coat, show horses need to be rugged. In some cases horses that have been clipped will develop unsightly cat hairs and for an early show it is then necessary to resort to the clippers again.

Regular grooming will keep the horse clean but attention must also be given to wisping.

Half an hour's hard work with a wisp each day, bringing the pad of hay down strongly on the neck, shoulders and quarters, does as much as anything for muscle development in those areas and will add immeasurably to the outline.

Exercise is best carried out at slow paces with a good long, half speed gallop being given the day before a show to take the itch out of the horse's heels. The more variation that can be introduced into the exercise period the better. With the horse bandaged in front and behind, a little work over cavalletti and even the odd jump or two will do no harm.

Grooming for the Show Ring —How the Pros Do It

By
GINA M. STATON

Grooming a horse's coat is only one part of the job. Good feeding and adequate exercise must also be included in the program.

Have you ever despaired because despite your best efforts, on horse show day your horse still didn't quite have that professional polish of the horses coming out of the big show stables? Have you ever wondered just what it is the professionals are doing differently, anyway? Here are some tips on how they do it, gathered over the years from the professional grooms themselves.

Of course, your first concern in grooming is with the horse's coat, and just as it takes months to train a horse, it takes months to get his coat in show shape, too. This doesn't mean that you have to spend hours every day toiling away; professionals with several horses to care for don't have that much time for each one, but it does mean you've got to plan ahead. You can't wait until the night before or even the week before a show to begin grooming for it.

A thorough grooming with brush and curry comb every day is a must as show day approaches. Use the curry comb—rubber or plastic but not metal—in a circular motion vigorously to loosen the dead hair and dirt next to the skin. Then use a stiff brush to remove what you've brought to the surface, followed by a soft brush for a final polish. Don't forget to pick out the feet and brush through the mane and tail, too.

Once a week when the weather is warm enough, shampoo your horse, preferably with a medicated shampoo that will fight skin fungus problems. When it's really hot and your horse is sweating a lot you'll probably have to wash him even more frequently. Pay particular at-

Horses are perfectly groomed and riders have been excused from wearing coats on this hot day in Florida.

tention to the roots of the mane and tail, where skin problems often begin, and don't forget to wash your horse's face where sweat accumulates under the bridle and halter. Don't use soap on the head, though; rather, wet his face thoroughly with a large natural sponge and then use your hand to vigorously rub behind his ears, around his eyes and on both sides of his muzzle. You might be surprised by how much old sweat and grime you'll lather to the surface this way. Then rinse completely with the wet sponge, not with a water hose directly in his face. Most horses really love this and it leaves the skin soft and clean. It's that accumulated sweat and dirt that makes horses rub their heads, which is how they acquire unsightly cuts and scratches.

When the horse is thoroughly clean and all the soap is rinsed out, remove the excess water with a sweat scraper or the side of your hand. Use only your hand on the legs where the skin is too thin to use a tool. Then walk the horse until dry. If you turn him loose, he'll roll!

Gray horses or horses with a lot of white will probably require a rinse of tail and legs with laundry blueing before a show to keep them from being a dingy yellow, but be cautious not to blister the skin with too strong a solution.

No matter how hard you work to groom and bathe your horse, though, the biggest difference in his appearance is made through the feed tub. Of course, he needs to be fed enough to stay in good flesh, but most of that shiny coat is a result of *what* he eats, too. A gleaming, dappled coat is the sign of robust health, and that means plenty of high-quality feed: a grain ration of probably 12% to 14%

One last polish before this pair is ready for the ring.

protein, good hay and usually a supplement on top of the feed for good measure. A supplement high in vitamin E will produce a good coat, and you can use one of the commercial mixtures, wheat germ oil, flax seed meal or even corn oil. Through the feed tub, dapples can be produced on practically any coat color, and they sure impress judges.

The professional stables also worm their horses frequently, some as often as every month. Even if a horse appears in good flesh, a low-level parasite infection robs him of that extra "bloom," and many owners notice a definite change in coat color following worming. And in the spring, worming often hastens the shedding out and growing of a new coat. Check with your veterinarian about a worming program suitable for your area, though, because worming products are toxic and need to be used with care.

Your everyday management plays an important role in getting your horse ready for the show ring, too. Make certain that there are no protruding or sharp objects in the stall or paddock on which the horse could cut himself, and you'll probably have to turn him out alone to prevent the playful kicks and bites that can blemish his coat.

During the summer months it will be necessary to keep your horse out of the hot sun so that his coat won't get bleached or sunburned. Many owners turn their horses out at night in the summer, unless mosquitoes are a severe problem. Keeping your horse out of the direct sun will also help keep him from sweating off a great deal of weight.

As cool weather approaches, most show stables start keeping a light sheet on their horses, at least at night, switching to a heavier blanket as it gets colder. This helps keep a horse from getting fuzzy and delays or eliminates the necessity of body clipping. Horses doing much work after they've grown a heavy coat really do need to be clipped because they're such a problem to cool out, but it takes a while for a clipped coat to look presentable again, so try to avoid it if you can. And remember, after you clip a horse you have no choice but to blanket him for the rest of the winter. If you find that you must body-clip, do it with a pair of large, heavy-duty clippers with a sharp blade, working against the direction the hair grows with long, even strokes.

Weekly clipping of the ears, bridle path and the long hairs on the chin and muzzle are routine for show stables, done of course with small, quiet clippers made for the purpose. The new cordless clippers with a rechargeable battery are a real help here since you aren't restricted to working within reach of an outlet. Patience pays off in clipping, and most horses will eventually learn to stand pretty quietly

Today most exhibitors serve as both rider and groom, but fathers make pretty good grooms, too.

for their weekly trim. Try stuffing a little cotton down in the ears before you begin with horses that are a particular problem to clip; it might be the noise they object to. Clip the hairs that overlap the coronet band with scissors and the fetlocks with body clippers about once a month.

Keeping manes and tails neat and in good condition is a regular task, too. They are usually brushed through with a slightly damp brush at every grooming, and a mane that persists in falling on the wrong side can be trained by dampening it and then braiding to the proper side overnight. Occasional application of creme rinse is useful on horses with very fine manes and tails, as is a little laundry blueing on grays that tend to yellow.

If a tail becomes badly matted, untangling it is a real chore. Most professionals start with a lot of creme rinse, carefully trying to work as much of the snarl out with their fingers as they can. If that doesn't work, the only recourse is to begin with a thin pocketknife blade, carefully slitting the matted hairs lengthwise. A lot of hair is lost this way but most of it will be dead anyway. When the matted hair is finally worked out, apply more creme rinse, brush through, and wrap the tail in a damp towel or bandage to smooth the frayed hairs. Once you've done this a few times you'll see why it's easier to keep up with it daily!

If your horse comes in after the summer and sheds out his bleached coat but still has a badly sunburned tail, you can cheat a bit and dye it back to a normal color. This procedure requires great care but it can be a real life-saver. Select one of the human products in a color just a bit darker than the tail naturally grows. Horse hair is a lot coarser than human hair, and it won't absorb the color as well. Be very careful that the horse doesn't flick any of the dye on his rump or flank, using a plastic bucket held well up under the tail during the entire procedure. Don't repeat the procedure too often, as it is hard on the hair and the skin, just as with humans.

Horses shown in the hunter classes are shown with their manes and often their tails braided, which means an extra chore on show day. The only way to learn to do a professional-looking braid job is with lots of practice. It isn't really necessary to braid the tail most of the time, and don't even attempt to do it for a show until you've mastered a professional tail job at home. Most grooms use either a blunt needle and heavy thread or yarn and a wire loop to braid with. Rubber bands really aren't suitable because the job simply won't stay neat-looking with them. Plan to braid the day of the show, not the night before, so that your braid job won't look frayed when the horse goes into the ring. A last-minute spritz with a little hair spray of the type that comes in a pump sprayer will hold any loose hairs nicely. Don't cut any stray hairs because the mane will be very uneven when you take it down.

Just before the horse goes into the ring, most grooms wipe a little vaseline or glycerine and rosewater inside the ears, around the eyes and on the muzzle to darken the skin and give it a soft appearance. This also keeps the skin from getting dry and flaky in these areas that are clipped regularly. Then a soft towel is quickly rubbed over the entire coat to remove any dust that has settled, and a thin coat of hoof dressing is painted on, most often a mixture of regular hoof dressing thinned with Neatsfoot Oil. Then a final check of the tack, a quick wipe over the rider's boots after he's mounted, and they are ready to go into the ring.

At most of the bigger shows you'll see the grooms lingering by the gate, a towel hanging out of a back pocket, waiting for their charges to finish the class. In the case of a class where the horses are first judged under saddle and then "stripped" to be judged on conformation, the grooms are often allowed to quickly run into the ring to help the exhibitor wipe off the saddle mark, the dust, and any saliva on the lips or chest. Then a few moments later, one of the grooms will proudly lead "his" horse back to the stable with a long blue ribbon fluttering from his bridle. To the professional groom, practically an extinct species, there is as much pride in turning out a horse beautifully for the show ring as there is for the rider who actually competes with him.

Most exhibitors today, however, serve as both rider and groom for their horses, so their pride in a ribbon of any color is double.

How to Make Take-Apart Jump Standards

By
GINA M. STATON

At a busy horse show, you'll welcome all the help you can get. The take-apart jump standard is a training aid guaranteed to make last-minute schooling a pleasure instead of a trial.

Tired of going to a horse show and finding just one schooling jump, with forty horses and riders waiting to use it? Or maybe you just don't have a lot of room to store jumps at home. You can solve both these problems with easy-to-make jump standards that come apart for storage—ideal for tossing in your trailer on show day.

To make a pair of four-foot standards, begin by gathering your materials. You will need:

- 2 four-foot lengths of 4 inch x 4 inch lumber for the uprights. These should be of straight, hard wood, not soft pine.
- 2 pieces of ⅝-inch or ¾-inch exterior-grade plywood, cut into three-foot squares.
- 8 short lengths of 4 inch x 4 inch lumber, each 15 inches long.
- 32 wood screws, 2½ to 3 inches long.
- 2 or 3 feet of aluminium electrical pipe about ¾-inch diameter.
- A wood saw.
- A hacksaw.
- A drill, with bits to drill the screw holes and for boring ¾-inch holes in the uprights.

Cut the lumber to the desired measurements, being careful that the cuts are straight, and sand as needed.

Next, mark the center of each piece of plywood by measuring in 18 inches from each side. Center one of the 4 x 4's upright over the mark, and trace around it. Take four of the short 4 x 4's and place these around, and slightly outside of, the square you have traced, leaving an open space in the center that will accommodate the upright of the standard. Adjust as needed so that the upright will slip in and out fairly easily, but will not wobble. Remember that a coat of paint will make the fit slightly tighter. There will be about an inch of plywood remaining on all sides after the braces are positioned.

Mark where the 4 x 4 braces are to be placed, and then turn over the plywood to secure the braces from underneath with four screws each, offset for security. Nails could be substituted but they are a real hazard if they should happen to work loose sometime later. Screws will hold more securely and are worth the extra time they take to install.

Now you have completed the braces and the upright of the jump standard, which will not be permanently fastened together. To use, simply slip the upright into the braces, and then take them apart again to store them.

Make the brackets to hold the jump rails by boring holes into the uprights, using a bit the same size as the aluminum pipe (about ¾ inch), and at an angle. Allow about four inches in your height measurement for the pole itself, so that for a rail set at three feet, the hole will be bored at 32 inches. Boring a hole every three inches is a good idea, but be sure all the holes are at the same angle. This is where using fairly hard wood is important, so that the holes will not have a tendency to open at the bottom from the weight of the rails, causing them to roll off too easily.

Make the pegs themselves by cutting the aluminum pipe into six-inch lengths with the hacksaw. Remove any burrs with a file. These pegs will be more durable than wooden pegs since they will not break off in the holes and will not bend unless given quite a hard rap. The pipe is inexpensive and a coffee can holds a generous supply.

Now simply construct the second standard in the same way, paint the pair, and they are ready for use. These standards will be extremely portable, inexpensive to construct, and quite serviceable.

LEARNING FROM THE EXPERTS

Rodney Jenkins wearing Leading Rider sash. *(Photo by Victor C. Lafrenz.)*

Horse Show Mistakes

By
HARLAN ABBEY

Some of the top trainers and judges tell of the frequent mistakes that can cost you a ribbon.

As riding becomes more popular, there are more and more horse owners who want to face the challenge of testing their riding ability or their horse's performance against others in horse show competition. Many of them begin by entering with little or no advance preparation or training, except for riding in the presence of a friend with more experience and later asking him: "What do you think?"

And since the friend usually is a friend first, and a horseman second, he often decides it is more tactful to say "You're doing great" than to give his frank opinion. Only after the novice showman has spent money for equipment, entry fees, stabling, and transportation does he find out that either he or his horse wasn't really ready to meet show competition.

Every rider or every horse can have an individual problem or two, but there are many mistakes that are common to many new riders just beginning to show. And most of them have been seen time and time again by the leading professional riders and trainers, who spend so much of their lives competing at the nation's large and small horse shows.

American Horseman recently interviewed several of the top English riders, trainers and judges to ask them which mistakes they have observed most often at different shows.

George Morris, a former Olympic rider who has since coached many top hunter and jumper riders and also has conducted clinics all over the world, believes the biggest problem with young show riders "is their desire to imitate some of the professional riders they see at shows. This is not a problem in some areas, where most professionals have had proper training when they were younger, but it can be disastrous when applied to some of the 'born' or 'natural' riders who never had the proper riding foundation yet win anyway because of their superior, in-born ability.

"This is less of a problem for hunter-jumper riders in the East than it is in the West. There are many exceptions, of course, but I would have to say that as a rule the Western hunter-jumper riders are the worst of any area of the country. They use such 'aids' as big roweled spurs and chain bits, which you'd never see at a major show in the East. When youngsters see 'so and so' using them, they're inclined to try them, too.

"Probably the worst fault children develop is rough hands. Hands can be almost hideous, as well as brutal, in their interference with a horse. But if a youngster never sees anyone with the kind, sympathetic hands you need, he will soon become rough with his own hands—because that is all he sees whenever he goes to a show.

"Another fault youngsters seem to drift into is to start 'sitting back' on a horse, getting their weight behind the vertical, and thus violating one of the principal rules of proper horsemanship. Again, they see the professionals riding like this, so they start to copy it. What they don't realize is that the pros are usually riding young, relatively unschooled horses most of the time, whether at home or at a show. These horses need to be given more guidance and ridden with more force than the child's older (usually), better educated horse.

"Another thing youngsters see going on at shows is the poling of jumpers—rapping them with a light bamboo pole between their coronet bands, just above their hooves, and the middle of their shins. This is a good training device, but only if used in moderation and if used the proper way.

"A good rider, an experienced amateur or professional, knows when a horse is jumping well and when he isn't. And if he does decide to pole his horse he knows how to ride him at a fence where a friend is holding a pole level with the top element in proper position. And he won't lose his position while the horse is being poled.

"But it makes you sick to see someone who really doesn't know what he's doing . . . they usually are interfering with their hands so the horse is getting jerked in the mouth and having his legs rapped at the same time.

"Another problem that soon arises, once a young rider starts to go to shows regularly, is that good riding is judged purely on the basis of ribbons and trophies won. This most often happens through the child's parents. We've all heard the term 'horse show parents,' and that is how that phrase developed, because of parents who want their children to ride well—which is only natural—but who equate good riding with blue ribbons.

"Once a child begins showing, his own competitive spirit and the reaction of show surroundings on himself and his horse give him plenty of pressure without the parents adding more on top of it all. They tend to inhibit their child's relaxation and progress. Many instruc-

George Morris, former Olympic rider, now a highly successful trainer and teacher. (Photo by Victor C. Lafrenz.)

tors refuse to let some parents even watch their child getting riding lessons!

"I once heard another instructor mutter, about a pupil's parents, 'All child riders should be born orphans!' But then I asked him, 'Who would pay the bills?' "

Dan Lenehan, one of the nation's most-respected judges of hunters, believes many young showmen appear ignorant of how to properly show a horse when he is being judged for conformation.

"If you watch the top professionals, you'll see they never stop showing a horse in a conformation class, they work every minute. Many others, once the judge has looked over their horse, seem to slump down into an 'it's over' attitude and let their horse get all sprawled out. Quite often I will look back at a horse to compare him to the one in front of me . . . and if he isn't posed properly he may lose a ribbon.

"One thing that doesn't impress me, and is done by many young riders who have seen some professionals do it, is holding the reins at the buckle, in one hand, in a non-jumping class.

"I like to see the rider having a little feel

Dave Kelley, veteran of many years in the show ring, is now in demand as a judge, also. (Photo by Victor C. Lafrenz.)

of the horse's mouth. The professionals frequently ride 'on the buckle' because the horse is so well balanced he doesn't have to be really 'ridden.' But when someone with less experience does it, this lackadaisical attitude gets overdone. The horse starts getting sloppy. He may not be doing anything wrong, but he's not performing right, either. I think riding with both hands on the reins makes a more appealing performance. Of course, if the horse's reins are slopping along his neck and he's the best mover in the ring, I won't hold it against him."

John Shaffner, owner of Hurdle Hill Farm in Lockport, N.Y., and a regular on the "A"-rated horse show circuit, believes lack of concentration is the biggest problem beginning show riders have, whether they are children or adults.

"You can have a 'green' (inexperienced) rider repeat back to you some last-minute instructions," he declared, "and then they'll go right into a ring and forget everything. You are lucky if they can even remember the order of fences they are going to jump.

"This pressure usually starts building as soon as they get to the show. They're excited, nervous, they want to talk to their friends, they worry about the different fences and the difference in the show ring. Then they want to school really well and there is just too much on their minds.

"Adults are subject to the same pressures—if they haven't shown as children—and are probably more self-conscious because of their ages. In addition, they have the nagging thought, 'Who'll cook the meals if I fall off and get hurt? '

"There is only one way to correct this problem and that is 'mileage': the more you ride and perfect your form, the less you have to concentrate on when you're in the ring, and the more shows you go to, the less you think about all the distractions and the more you can concentrate on riding well and showing your horse.

"In an equitation class, many young riders are simply too loose in the saddle. Sometimes this is tension. Instead of getting really deep into the saddle and sitting 'into' the horse, the riders tighten up their muscles—thinking they're strengthening their grip—but instead they are squeezing themselves up further on top of the horse, almost into a ball. The more you are 'into' the horse, the more you can feel what he is doing, or about to do.

"Many beginning equitation riders, in a class over fences, can eliminate themselves as soon as they go into a ring. Some make a sloppy, irregular circle on their approach to the first fences—and some don't even circle, just rush at the fence. This, again, is due to lack of concentration.

"I also think the most common fault I see in equitation class is a lack of use of the legs and too much use of the hands. Judges are looking for a fluid performance, with no rough movements. I try to teach young riders how to keep a 'feel' of the horse's mouth from becoming a 'vise'-grip.

"Then, on the other hand, there are the youngsters who trust their horses too much. Just because your horse has jumped a fence in the schooling area, or in the first class, doesn't mean he will do it every time. You can't simply drop your hands down on his neck two or three strides from a fence and 'trust' him to get over. You have to support him with your legs and hands right into the take-off point. Once a horse is in the air, you could cut the reins right off the bridle—but you'll never get in the air if the horse doesn't leave the ground.

"When a horse refuses a fence, many inexperienced riders take him back 50 to 100 feet and run him back to it. Speed doesn't make a horse jump. It would be better if the fence was three feet or three-and-a-half feet high, to go back about 15 feet or so, support the horse well with hands and legs, be sure he sees the fence, and ride him over it.

"When riders get more experience, they don't make as many basic mistakes, but often develop other new, bad habits. Some begin getting too high out of the saddle over fences, or begin ducking their heads to one side over one fence and then maybe to the other side over the next fence. The whole secret of riding in hunter and horsemanship classes is to try to make every fence 'ride' the same way.

"Many riders, over a course of three-and-a-half-foot fences, ask a horse to stand back too far from the jump instead of riding him to within three-and-a-half feet from the fence, which will make a more natural, fluid jump. These riders have not yet developed an eye for distance, they don't know how to steady their horses between fences. They do know if they ride their horse strongly into the fence that he'll jump it—they hope.

"They don't think eight 'nice' fences, they think it's better to stand back and try for 'big' fences. Again, this is lack of concentration or experience.

"Years ago, if a rider didn't want to spend the time working on proper riding form for equitation and hunter classes but had a pretty good 'natural seat,' he would enter jumper classes. The courses they were building then were just a bunch of fences that you could ride at, get over, and win a ribbon.

"Today the courses are a lot more complicated in jumper classes. There are fences in combination, changes of distances on the different lines of the course . . . you have to have better control of your horse, so you have to learn to sit quieter, use your aids a lot quicker and smoother, and generally be a more polished rider."

Steve Hawkins, member of a distinguished family of horsemen, judges often with his brother, Arthur, or his father, Frank. When it comes to a point where a judge's decision is to be questioned, Steve maintains that the child never should be allowed to approach the judge unless he is accompanied by a parent or another adult.

"This questioning should come immediately after the class—if possible—while everything is fresh in the judge's mind. You should know the child's or horse's number and you might describe the horse by coat color. Bring the child along, by all means.

"I've found that if the child comes up to the judge alone, what the judge tells him is usually completely misunderstood or is interpreted improperly. Then the child will continue to make the same mistakes. It would be much better, especially at smaller shows, to have time to have a question-and-answer session after each equitation class.

"It is also my belief that no child rider can reach the point where he can win at the nation's largest shows unless he is coached by a top-flight professional. A parent, no matter how excellent a horseman he is, just cannot do the job. Many leading professionals even send their children to take lessons from other professionals.

"You send a child to a professional instructor for the same reasons you send him to school, to be instructed by someone who knows more about a subject than his parents, and also to expose the child to a different adult personality."

Dave Kelley, a top-ranking trainer and rider for many years and now much in demand as a judge as well, has a unique philosophy of showing:

"I believe a horse show must emphasize the word 'show.' We professionals are showing our horses and our training methods to the future show ring riders or others who may be buying horses from us at some time in the future. I think you, as an exhibitor, have to come prepared to put on a show for the spectator.

"By that I mean your horse must be ready for the show and you should show him in a dignified way. For that reason, I don't believe that if a horse makes a mistake—such as a refusal at a fence—you drop everything and start beating on the horse and spurring and whipping him around the rest of the course . . . what we call a 'cowboy round.'

"First of all, you're hurting the horse. Every round is part of his education, a reference for his next round. One bad, rough round will be remembered. Also, you're leaving a poor impression of that horse in the minds of your judges, your fellow professionals and prospective buyers. They are going to remember that 'cowboy round' the next time they see you and your horse.

"For the same reason, I believe when you enter a show you are signing a contract to show before a certain judge. If you don't like the way he pins one particular class, that's no excuse to stop showing in front of him. If you enter a show, you show in it all the way through, except in a case of injury. If you don't want to accept that certain judge's opinion of your horse or your riding, then show someplace else."

Rodney Jenkins, the winningest hunter-jumper rider in the country with a string of top horses that can number 20 or more at a single show, has a "pet peeve: equitation," and he explains:

"To me, the worst thing you can do with a young rider is constantly drill, drill and drill him in various exercises to correct various position faults. Pretty soon the child is afraid to move at all, to do anything wrong.

"Position and style on a horse's back are important, but not all-important. Everyone has one natural way of riding and any change that is too radical will hurt it."

Riding four and five horses in one class may fatigue the average rider, just to think about it, but Rodney believes it an advantage. He notes:

"I think the most common mistake I see show riders make—no matter how much experience they have—is getting 'stage fright.' So many of them, once they enter the ring, appear to want to get the round over as soon as possible. They seem to forget everything they know.

"No one seems to ride as well in the show ring or the outside course as he does in the schooling ring, where he is really concentrating on his horse and the fence ahead. Perhaps it's because I ride three or four horses in each class and know if I make a mistake in my first round I have a couple of chances to correct it, but—although I'd be the last to say winning isn't important—one has to realize it's not 'life or death' out in the ring. And if you feel tense, the horse is going to feel it and he's going to get tense, too.

"This is shown by riders not keeping their horses 'together,' collected . . . not taking the time to think things out. They seem to ride with an attitude of getting the round over with as soon as possible. That's the wrong way to go about it.

"Another common mistake made by many riders who have only one horse to show is to enter too many classes. Even in a one-day show, I don't think you can show a horse in both the hunter and jumper classes. Unless it's an unusual horse, that is just too much to do. What riders forget is it isn't just the number of classes but in most jumper classes there will be one or two—or maybe three—jump-offs. So instead of riding in, for example, three hunter classes and three jumper classes you actually are putting your horse around a course of jumps eight to ten or twelve times, not just six times."

"Rapping" or "poling" a horse with a light bamboo pole is an art that few horsemen can do correctly, Jenkins contends. "You've got to hit him between the coronet band and the middle of his shins. If you hit him too high up on his shins, he'll react by bringing his lower legs back underneath his body, which forces his knees further down. And if you rap him on his hooves, he doesn't feel it.

"You can't just swing at his legs, either. That will get the horse jumping flat, not arching himself properly. Have your assistant hold the pole behind and level with the top rail of the practice jump. Then, when the horse jumps, have him lift it, hold it steady, and let the horse move into it.

"But, like any other training device, it can be overdone. Some horses, usually the rather phlegmatic kind, might need it quite frequently. High-strung horses might become undone if they are poled."

George Morris on Riding Style

With a wide range of knowledge, heightened by many experiences in International competition, one of America's most famous horsemen talks about equitation judging.

The first thing which must be considered when you are judging any competition is the execution and performance in solving the given problems. When riding in equitation classes on the flat, you must execute the walk, trot, canter, the sitting trot, counter canter, hand gallop and the back, as well as turns on the forehand and haunches. You *have* to *execute* the movements.

But in the very good shows where competition reaches the highest levels, the performance in itself is *not* enough. You almost take for granted that the performance will be there. You expect that all the competitors will walk, trot and canter with sufficient impulsion, that the horses will be pretty well on the bit and will bend in the proper directions, that the turns on the forehand and haunches will be accomplished—that they will execute the performance. Therefore, what you must then judge are the *qualities* that each rider possesses. His feel, his balance, his basic correctness in seat and overall position, his *validity* or *quality* as a rider.

A rider such as Billy Steinkraus will execute a ride on the flat or over fences beautifully, and his *quality* and his *basics* are excellent, too. However, you might present another rider with the same flat test or jumping round, and while he or she might execute it practically as well (or as well), his *qualities* as a rider are not as good. He might not be able to get along with as many horses because perhaps he is an over-rider and a little cruder; not necessarily rough or inadequate, but simply lacking the ultimate finesse and complete harmony with the horse.

One of my pet peeves or favorite topics for discussion is judging which ignores the basic qualities of a ride and considers only the execution. If you take a class over jumps such as the Maclay or Medal Finals in which the courses are pretty straightforward and not overly difficult, you may have anywhere between 15 and 25 riders who execute those courses very, very well, and just about the same. Now through the process of elimination you sort out the 15 to 25 competitors who are able to execute and solve the problems on a very good and almost equal basis. During the judging of the execution you MUST, in my opinion, be judging the *qualities* of each rider. Is he riding *invisibly* with the motion of the horse, which is much harder than sitting back and driving over the course and showing the ride? Does he have a *soft* quality when asking a horse for an increase or a decrease or a turn? Is his quality *soft* and *smooth* and *sympathetic* or does he simply execute the ride? As this rider is performing over the course does he have the kind of a leg and the position of a leg that could be *independent* and *strong* on a *stopper* and *independent* and *light* on a *rusher*? This is what I mean when I talk about "basics" and *basic qualities* of a rider. I think that sometimes in good equitation classes, judges don't pay enough attention to, or are not sufficiently aware of, the basics and qualities essential to a rider of great versatility: one who is able to ride a hot horse as well as a stopper; one who can cope with any situation because of his foundation.

If you watch a group of riders execute a course well and, as a judge you go to the one who is behind the motion, you are very likely choosing an *over-rider* who, if he is asked to ride a hot horse or a sensitive horse, will be too strong in that horse's back. So in selecting a rider who is behind the motion; in choosing BEHIND versus WITH the motion, you are picking out a quality that is not very versatile. That's getting down to basics in riding qualities. One of my principle objectives with a rider is developing his ability to ride softly, in balance, in the middle of the horse over the center of gravity, not always having to ride behind the horse because he feels more comfortable sitting down and back behind the motion. And I repeat that when you go to that over-rider who is very, very deep and behind and who is sitting a little heavy on his horse, he'll irritate some horses, he'll over-ride some horses, he's got to drop back a little early and a little more often than the rider who is nicely galloping over the center of his horse.

So, a rider who is distinctly behind the horse's motion, even though he gets the jumps and gets the performance and executes the round as well as the one who is with the motion, has to be considered a less able rider and a less versatile rider than the one who is with the motion of his ride.

If somebody executes a round and his toes are out too far, he is going to someday run into a horse that will find that leg too *grippy* and respond accordingly. If in his basic riding qualities he is toeing in too much, someday he

George Morris, one of the foremost instructor/riders on the horse show scene today, brings to his teaching an extensive range of knowledge heightened by his experiences in international competition. (Photo by Budd.)

is going to run into the problem of not having a tight and strong enough leg. This is what I mean when I say that these basic qualities will catch up with a rider, and when you are judging I believe you must consider very strongly, discern quickly and accurately, and attach great importance to basic riding qualities, habits and foundations.

If a rider has a wonderful round but he doesn't look around his turns early enough, that seemingly minor fault will catch up with him at some time and he is going to have a late turn. What I'm getting at is that when we are judging those 15 to 25 finalists who have put up comparable outstanding performances on that given day, we must go beyond the realm of correctness of execution. There is no question about using this group as the one from which the six or eight ultimate ribbon winners will be selected, but as we are judging them let us not be satisfied with just the accomplishment of the required movements. That's what I think judges sometimes miss as they become increasingly awed at a continuing high level of

George Morris has coached countless Medal and Maclay winners. Former pupil Katie Monahan won the Maclay in 1968 and the AHSA Medal in 1972. *(Photo by Budd.)*

achievement such as might be seen in the Finals. They forget to search out the nuances and refinements of truly outstanding riding or to clearly define the flaws and estimate their consequences. They do not ask themselves where the leg fault that this rider has is going to catch up with him, or whether that hand fault can cause more serious problems with different horses under different circumstances. They do not evaluate the seriousness of a given basic fault, and in some instances seem to ignore it entirely.

A poor basic habit which some riders are exhibiting now is too much of a release; a throw-away release with their hands about half way up the horse's crest. For an advanced equitation rider that's too much of a move. It's going to catch up with him and some day drop his horse on his forehand causing him to hang a leg. That basic quality flaw should be penalized even if he has a wonderful round.

The basic quality of being round and weak-backed will tell on a rider when he needs his back to drive a hesitator or a stopper down to a large or difficult fence. Let us penalize such a rider for this basic inadequacy.

In judging equitation now, we have got to go back to a little bit of the old days, say 10 or 15 years ago, and look beyond the execution of those eight jumps. We must make a more careful scrutiny of the rider and see what he really is on the basis of his inherent riding qualities—his balance, his tact, his sympathy, his ability to over-ride or under-ride a situation as the circumstances demand. These are qualities which you can discern in a split second while you are judging a round and in my opinion they should weigh heavily on and be reflected in a rider's score. I think it is very risky for the development of our riding and our riders for the future to ignore these foundations and cornerstones of good riding just because a specific set of commands, tests or courses were executed promptly, precisely and on the whole, quite well.

In teaching and showing we are dealing with the average rider. There are very few Rodney Jenkins', David Broome's or Bill Steinkraus' even though we occasionally do see a display of unusual talent. So what we are doing when we teach, and again it is the basics, we are teaching the most economical and easiest way to accomplish something. Take Bernie Traurig for example. His leg is quite far in front of his body but *he* can jump well that way. Take an average rider and put his leg in same position and he's going to get left back, he's going to drop back in the air, he's not going to be with his horse because his timing isn't there yet. This is a very good case in point of function following form. Form in this instance, for the average rider, places his leg under his body by the back edge of the girth. That's where he can function and use his leg most economically and easily and therefore, most effectively. You always have to give the form (i.e. position) first. You've got to give the *physical* before the *feel.* The feel is *not* physical. The feel is emotional.

Here I would draw a parallel to acting. You can't get the feel of a scene until you physically do the scene. After you have physically gone through the blocking, and said the words and related to the other person in just straight speech, then you start feeling what that scene is all about. It is just the same with a rider. When you put the form on him he starts feeling the way it is right. If you put it on him wrong he'll start feeling how to do it wrong and you'll not get anywhere.

When considering the basic riding qualities essential to success in the equitation division (or any division), you cannot disregard the schooling demands which today's courses place upon the horses. With the possible exception of a very long, open outside course, every hunter round, every equitation round, every jumper round requires a *computerized* ride. That means that everything from the start to the finish including the turns, the distances in between jumps, the approach to jumps, the way you approach different lines of jumps—verticals versus oxers versus combinations—is a computerized program that you work out very much as a rule before you enter the ring.

You put it into the computer *before* you enter the ring. You can almost say that hunter rides in a ring are more computerized than jumper rides because jumper rides offer several options to most obstacles, and you can still win the class. Hunter riding with the distances that are employed—72 feet, 84 feet, whatever; the striding—six, seven, eight or two strides—is now so measured that there is no question of winning the class in three strides, four strides or five strides, which you could do with a jumper. You have got to do it the way the other competitor does it. If he does five and she does five, then you have got to do five to win or get a good ribbon. Rarely can you violate the computer and still come out on top, or even in contention.

This boils down to more and more obedience, discipline, manners and schooling of the horse. That is where those who have in the past, and still might use a tranquilizer have a little edge because they have a quieter and frequently more obedient horse to work with. Sometimes it backfires on them and they come up with a

Buddy Brown, another Morris pupil, won the ASHA Medal in 1973 and went on to become one of the youngest members of the USET. *(Photo by Budd.)*

dead or dull horse and he doesn't react well and he blows it. But keeping it on the schooling level and not on the medication level, this is where, from beginning to end, you have got to be a trainer of the horse. You can't expect a horse who is only a good jumper to get it done. You must be able to control his stride almost to the inch. Not to the foot, but to the inch! You must be able to shorten him to the inch, lengthen him to the inch. He can't anticipate a turn, cut a turn or bulge a turn. He must have a mouth—a nice mouth—so that when you ask him to come back it's invisible. He has to respond to the leg so that when you ask him to increase and lengthen it is invisible, and it has to happen instantaneously. It is a nice evolution because this is where good dressage, natural dressage, hunter/jumper dressage is coming into focus. The people who cater to that kind of development of a horse and rider have an edge. It is getting to be impossible to compete with any hope of success without that training. Many people use the term *dressage*. Others use the phrase to *school your horse*. Still others say *get him broke*. It doesn't matter what you call it, they all mean the same thing—obedience; instant, invisible, smooth obedience. Obedience that is jerky and abrupt and obvious simply won't do. Obedience that isn't instantaneous won't do. Lack of obedience is tantamount to failure. In order to have the execution of the performance on the part of the rider you must have the basics—the basics of reflexive obedience—on the part of the horse.

Therefore, in order to even compete on the upper levels of competition you have got to have the basics of the horse and the rider and the execution of the performance. Then it comes down to the evaluation of basic qualities of the rider in equitation (as already discussed) or of the horse, which in a hunter class, for example, might include comments such as: "he's not as good a mover as the other horse," "over this fence he was not as tight with his front end" or "at that fence he had a rub." Then you are getting into sophisticated, specific judging which is also very high calibre judging.

So when competition reaches the higher levels we see that execution and performance are nearly always taken for granted, and it is actually the degree and the perfection, the art and the beauty of the execution which are being judged and are, in fact, the deciding factors.

How to Show Your English Pleasure Horse

By
MARY ANN SEBREY

There are special English pleasure classes for Saddlebred, Arabian and Morgan, and subtle differences among them. Here are some pointers on how to show in each of them.

The American Saddlebred is the original English pleasure horse, the pride of Southern gentlemen who wanted an easy-gaited mount.

But today, owners of many other breeds enter English pleasure classes all across the country. Versatile breeds like Morgans and Arabians seem to adapt readily to the elegant saddle seat style of riding. There are Arab and Morgan English pleasure classes at most major shows, and many open English pleasure classes at smaller shows.

How can you do the best job of showing your English pleasure horse, whether he's a Saddlebred, a Morgan or an Arabian? Here are some tips by two successful amateurs who have shown extensively in English pleasure classes.

Mrs. Alicia Davis of Gainesville, Fla., is a working mother who has successfully shown her own Saddlebred mare, Southern Rambler (Penny). Alicia gave Penny her basic training and with the help of Saddlebred trainer Dewey Henderson, prepared her for a show career. Penny was 1972 and 1973 South Carolina American Saddlebred Pleasure Horse Champion. She was 7th out of 81 entries at the Kentucky State Fair Horse Show World's Championship in 1972, and reserve English Pleasure Champion at Montgomery, Ala., against all breeds of pleasure horses in a class of 50.

Alicia also showed the Morgan mare Double M Velvet Lass, owned by Metta Baxter of Newberry, Fla., to Top Ten in two divisions at the Morgan Grand National Show in 1974.

Velvet was never out of the ribbons in her first year of showing.

Sandy Jones, a Gainesville teenager, showed her half-Arab, Longlane Sundance, at the Southern Regional 4-H Horse Championship, and the gelding earned the title of 4-H Overall English High Point Horse. With Alicia's help, Sandy trained her horse, which she purchased as an unbroken three-year-old. Sandy has also won in English pleasure at All-Arab and open shows and was twice first place and twice reserve in the saddle seat division at Alachua County 4-H shows.

You don't need the most expensive horse, tack or attire to show your horse well, both Alicia and Sandy agreed. If you make the best of what you have, you can be successful. A large part of showing in English pleasure is the pleasurable appearance you and your horse make.

Your horse will make a better appearance if he looks and feels his best. He should be in good health and good physical shape. The horse with decent conformation, a pleasant disposition and a nice way of moving will always make a better showing.

There's not much you can do to change your horse's conformation, but good grooming can transform the appearance of any breed of horse.

By all means, your horse should be clean when you go into the ring. Pay special attention to his white markings, if he has any, and scrub till they're gleaming white. Trim his ears, fetlocks and muzzle—nothing looks worse than a shaggy horse. If your horse has grown a winter coat before the first spring shows, you might want to body-clip him. If so, do it at least a month ahead of time, so the hairs will have time to grow a little and blend together. Have your horse's feet trimmed or shod.

Before you saddle up for your class, brush and rub your horse's coat till it shines and apply hoof-black if he has dark hooves.

These extra touches may take time and advance planning, but if you ride a gleaming horse into the ring you'll attract everyone's attention, including the judge's.

The same goes for tack. Proper, clean tack will make you appear professional.

Both Arabian and Morgan riders have adopted the Saddlebred's "clothing" as correct for showing in English pleasure classes. A double bridle with a lightweight snaffle bit and a curb bit are usual, Alicia said. Occasionally Morgan owners will be seen showing with a Pelham bit with long curb shanks, so that it resembles a double bridle.

Any type of flat saddle is acceptable, Alicia said, although a cut-back show saddle probably shows the horse off best, especially a high-headed Saddlebred. Sandy has shown her half-Arab using a dressage saddle. In general, Alicia said, the bulkier the saddle, the heavier it will look on the horse and the more it will take away from his overall appearance.

Be sure all your tack is clean and in good repair. The bridle should fit correctly and all the straps should be in their keepers. If your bridle has a new piece, oil it so it will match the rest, Alicia pointed out. A new piece of yellow leather will stand out like a sore thumb.

As for your own attire, a well-fitting saddle suit, derby, jodhpur boots and gloves should be worn. Your clothing need not be expensive. A homemade saddle seat outfit, Alicia said, can even look better than a bought one because it can be tailored to fit exactly. Conservative colors are still the rule. Pick a color that will complement your horse's coat. Some people prefer a suit with a jacket of contrasting color—for example, blue, red or green, worn with black jodhpurs and black accessories. But flashy colors are frowned upon. The idea is to make a pleasant picture.

Your clothing and hair should be clean and neat. Girls should wear makeup, perhaps even a little more than they usually do, so they don't look "dead."

One last note: "Always wear gloves," Alicia said.

Now you and your horse are ready to enter the ring. You can still make or break your performance by what you do—or don't do—to show your horse to his best advantage.

About half of the game is attitude. "If you ride meekly," said Alicia, "you'll win meekly. Look like you're enjoying it and know what you're doing."

It is difficult for a tense, nervous rider to convey the impression that his horse is giving him a pleasurable ride, although Sandy admits, "It's hard to get in there without being nervous."

Remember that you're showing from the moment you enter the ring till you go up to get your ribbon, Alicia advised. Position yourself in the ring to your best advantage. "You want to be able to show your horse. Don't get covered. Make your pass with no one around you."

Stay away from unruly horses and horses that are doing extremely well. Don't put yourself right next to a really super horse unless you think you're better. It will only make you look worse.

Don't be afraid to circle around to get into a better position. If you're trotting, for example, and the judge calls for a walk, you're perfectly within your rights to keep on trotting past a pack of horses before you slow to a walk. And when the judge asks for a canter, you don't have to respond instantly. Instead, take the time to set your horse up properly, then canter.

The judge will know you're making an effort to show your horse, and after all, that's what it's all about.

If a piece of equipment breaks, you can feel free to come to the center of the ring and correct the problem.

No matter what breed of horse you ride, the judge will be looking for the same basic things in an English pleasure horse. Sandy said: "He's looking for nice, pleasurable horses. Your horse should look like a good family horse. You should act as if you're both having a pleasurable ride. He should be nice and calm and willing to do what you ask of him."

Alicia said the pleasure horse should have "pleasurable gaits, be attractive, set up, working nicely, not fighting, comfortable." He should also be well-mannered and make his gait transitions easily.

In Saddlebred pleasure classes and in many Morgan classes, judges look for "a lot of motion up front," Alicia said.

The Saddlebred pleasure horse should give the appearance of a spirited but controlled mount. He should never be "diving" into the bridle at any gait; he should be ridden on light contact. His walk should be square and straight, but the Saddlebred should always have higher motion than a Morgan pleasure horse. He should display a good, strong trot without sacrificing form. The Saddlebred's canter should be very smooth and comfortable-looking.

The Morgan pleasure horse will be asked to display both a regular and extended trot. His walk should be brisk and flat-footed. The judge looks for speed in an extended trot, and a horse that uses his legs, but again, without appearing out of form. His canter should be steady, relaxed, collected.

"But don't get so carried away with slowness that he walks behind," Alicia advised.

The Arab or half-Arab should display the lower-going motion that is natural to his breed, Sandy explained. His walk should be flat-footed and he should be ridden on a light rein. His normal trot is slow and airy; his extended trot covers ground without using a lot of up-and-down motion. His canter should be slow, easy and smooth. The Arab is often asked to hand-gallop, which is just slightly faster than a canter and is ridden on a light rein.

Every English pleasure horse, no matter what breed he is, must back correctly. He should back straight and steadily, not necessarily rapidly, and without head-tossing. In the line-up, he should stand correctly. (Morgans and Saddlebreds "stretch.") He should be kept alert.

Any English pleasure horse, though calm, should always be alert. He should never look "dead" or "doggy," with sour ears that spell boredom.

To help keep her horses fresh and alert, Alicia varies their activity. She doesn't ride every day, but sometimes drives the horses or just turns them out to play. Trailriding is another good way to keep a horse from becoming ring-sour.

Sandy advises, "Get your horse in the ring for experience" at lots of small shows. She took her horse to many 4-H shows where she could compete against kids her own age.

"Get to where you and your horse can really work together," Sandy said.

Alicia suggests dressage training to increase your horse's responsiveness. She also suggests seeking the advice of a more experienced horseman when you need help.

Every person who is showing should remember, Alicia added, that "It's just this man's opinion—what this man likes. One judge may love your horse; another may not."

In the game of showing, "You pay your money, you take your chances," she said.

The Rusty Gait

By
MARIAN BOND

Hands, seat and legs, and keeping the weight in the right place, make up the proper combination for the rider when showing the hunter in flat or jumping classes, in the view of trainer Rusty Stewart. Rusty, who does not use voice commands, stated that preparing a hunter required a lot of time, good experiences and good riders. And to do really well a horse should have the ability to relax and respond, not through fear or pressure, but because he is asked to respond.

One of the first things Stewart likes to do when a young horse comes into his training facility is to watch him in the jumping chute. "I can turn the horse loose in there and watch him jump without him worrying about a rider on his back. He doesn't have to do anything but jump," the California trainer explained. He said that the first time they might be a little confused, but he will have them jump 10 or 12 fences. This he will do for two or three days, asking them to jump a little higher fence each day. "They learn how to do it by themselves, and when a rider gets on them and trots them down to a fence for the first time, at least they have a basic idea of what they're supposed to do."

The jumping chute at Stewart's Winrock Farms is 40x90, and they choose this size because one person can stand in the center with a longeing whip and keep a horse going. Any larger, and two people would be required in the chute. Rusty said that they do not use a longe line at this work because it would be something else for the horse to worry about.

The horse's concentration can be keyed only to jumping the fences. The lane in the jumping chute is 12 feet wide, and the sides are 8 feet high, so the horses cannot see out and become distracted. The jumps in the chute are a cross rail and a vertical one on one side and a 24-foot combination on the other side with a parallel jump or square fence. And these high-spirited young horses don't need much encouragement to begin their work.

"This matter of keeping their attention is important," Stewart said. "Especially in starting a green horse. Babies have a tendency to let their minds wander. It's hard to keep their attention. Another important thing I teach them in the chute is not to be frightened if a rider loses the stirrups." For this training, Rusty will put a horse in the chute with a saddle on and let the stirrups flap on their sides as they go around and over the jumps. "They get to realize that running away is not going to do any good. You try to instill this confidence and trust in them. They trust you and try to respond to what you ask. And it takes time. With young horses there can be no certain pattern. For instance, some horses would not be bothered by stirrups. So we don't do this with every horse. Just the ones that I feel would need it." Rusty said that when they are getting young green horses ready for their first shows, they try to find out all the little things that bother them and work on them. "Then you go to the shows and you find out a lot more," he said.

At Winrock Farms the bitting rig is often used in the training of the horses, and they like to longe the horse in the rig. For this they use elastic side reins, and the forward motion of the horse makes these reins pull against the side of his mouth.

It was pointed out that this work should be done gradually. This is particularly helpful if a horse is a little rank because he eventually learns that he is only fighting himself and does not associate this situation with a rider. Another problem that is helped with this kind of work is a horse that might be a little hard in the mouth. Done properly, this will soften his mouth and make him more responsive. The trainer finds that for some horses the bitting rig is only required in the initial training, while for others it is necessary to go back to this tool frequently.

Rusty can tell a lot about how a horse is jumping by the way he feels during the jump. "If he's relaxed, if he uses his head, neck and back, an experienced rider can tell basically by the way he feels. You can tell when a horse hangs a leg or doesn't use his back properly. It is obvious. You know it doesn't feel right." Nevertheless, Stewart strongly believes that a trainer needs a ground man. "And there are a lot of reasons," he said. "Although a horse feels really good in the air and like he's doing everything right, it's all the little things, technical things that the rider cannot tell."

Stewart explained that, at the top of the arc, the horse's knees should be right together. This is one thing the man on the ground will look for. He will watch to see how the horse uses his hind end. "He's not supposed to pull it up under him. You more or less want him to flip his hind end out," he said.

"Your legs are the most important as far as your aids go," he continued. "Your seat and your legs are your gas pedal. Squeeze your legs and sit down harder. This leaves one direction open for the horse, and that is forward.

"Basically, during the jump the rider should just stay in good balance with the horse so he doesn't impair the horse's jumping ability or style. The rider should squeeze the horse off the ground unless it is a strong horse that is in the bridle and wants to be a little keen. This horse you would just ask him off. Ask him to leave the ground. Every horse is so different. And many horses, because of their own intelligence and experience, may then hit the fence on the proper stride and it would just happen, particularly on your well-trained horses. On your green horses, you don't fall asleep on them when you're taking them over the fences.

"As the horse starts to go up the rider starts to bend down, so that when the horse is at the top of the arc, the rider's back should be about parallel to the horse's neck. The weight of the rider should be on the leg line. A lot of people lean on their hands during the jump. That would be something that we would want to correct. A horse cannot come off the ground if a person has their body weight on their front end. The weight should be in the middle of the horse, not forward, certainly not on the back end, and not to either side. The horse leaves the ground from its hindquarters. They rock back and push off the ground and the back end flips out."

Concerning hand position, Rusty said that he likes to see very light contact with the horse's mouth, so that he can drop his head and neck down. "During the jump your hand moves slightly and at the top of the arc it makes a parallel line with the rider's back and the horse's neck. The arm is just lightly there. The leg is kept fairly perpendicular to the ground, with the body weight balanced there. As the horse returns to the ground, the rider gradually, while maintaining that important balance, returns to the seat."

Rusty remarked that the stride is important, as is riding each horse to the proper takeoff point. "This all depends on how high the fence is," he said. "For a 3-foot jump you would want to take off 3 feet in front of it and land 3 feet the other side of it. For a 6-foot fence you would take off 6 feet in front; and for a 5-foot jump you would take off 5 feet before. If you jump a 4-foot fence and he leaves the ground 3 feet before the jump, he is not going to have a real round arc. He will take off short of the fence and he will carry out that extra foot on the other side. You want their arc right over the top of the fences.

"Your older, experienced horses have pretty good judgment and they can figure out the right strides. But the rider must be good. On the young horses it is the rider and his eye that gets the horse to the correct spot, and then gives the signal to leave the ground. Timing, coordination and depth perception are most important. They are the basics that the rider has to develop and they are things that are hard to teach. They come from experience; doing it."

Rusty finds that with the aid of the jumping chute, he is able to start the horses in this phase of training while they are still working on the basic lessons on the flat. But generally, before a horse is taken to the chute, he likes them to know a large portion of the basics. They should be pretty well balanced and know how to turn and bend real well.

The trainer likes a horse to carry his head down and out. "If a horse is tense, his neck will have a tense, straight line. And so I work with the horse to try and get it as relaxed and as quiet as possible. If you can get them to do what you ask without their feeling pressured, it just follows that their head and neck will be relaxed. Some horses may never relax as much as you would want them to. Sometimes an owner will get anxious and say that a certain horse has been shown before, so he wants him shown. Even though I might want to spend a little more time, I might have to go ahead and show a horse that had not relaxed to the point I would like." Rusty agreed that if a person has a horse with a reputable trainer, that person should follow the trainer's suggestions concerning the training of that horse.

To be a good hunter, a horse does not necessarily have to be a Thoroughbred, but generally the requirements are met best by Thoroughbreds because they are big and athletic. The trainer said that a hunter should have a nice sloping shoulder with prominent withers and a nicely shaped neck. The head should be in proportion to the rest of the body, not too small. It should be fine and show quality. The eyes should be well set apart, open looking and big.

He likes to use a full cheek snaffle and he also uses a copper snaffle. He said that some horses like the taste of the copper bar and some do not. The full cheek snaffle helps when you want to keep them straight or in turning them. Rusty uses a martingale on a horse as long as it is needed, but he likes to go to the show without a martingale whenever possible. He pointed out, however, that some horses will always need one.

Rusty likes to start a horse in the hunter training at around the age of three, but this also depends on their size and how mature they are as far as bone structure. "Some, maybe, you won't start until they are four or five. Some you might start on the flat when they are two."

When he is working with a young horse that is getting excited and rushing up to the jumps, he likes to sit as quietly as possible on him and do a lot of turning and stopping. "If you felt the horse start to get strong two strides in front of the fence, and all the time he's waiting for you to tell him, and he's anticipating the fence and starting to get strong in front of it, you might even want to start again over a little cross rail. You don't want them charging up. You want them to come up on a nice smooth even pace."

You can never anticipate exactly what is going to happen at a show when you take a young horse. Stewart will sometimes longe a horse after they get to a show, or get on him and walk him around and relax him as much as possible. "Some horses, the crowds and other things distract them. They walk in the ring and know what they have to do. But somebody is liable to cough in the stands and that might distract them. There are different things that you don't have at home, like people standing around the rail. You know pretty much whether you have the horse right, whether you have been schooling him properly. But you never know what is going to happen at a show. There are no guarantees."

Train Your Show Horse to Win

By
CHUCK TYLER

California has, for many years, been one of the most popular training grounds for halter and performance horses. Among the top trainers in the state is Ralph Corpe, head of Western training at Coto de Caza Equestrian Center, located in the Santa Ana Mountains about forty miles south of Los Angeles.

Corpe literally was born into the horse business some fifty-one years ago. His father, Guy R. Corpe, has been a prominent quarter horse breeder for more than half a century, starting before the quarter horse registry was founded in 1940.

"As a boy, I had to ride anything my father would buy or trade, either at our ranch in El Monte, or the second spread in Sacramento, California," Corpe recalls. "Sometimes it would be an ill-tempered, bad-acting stallion, or the next day it would be a gentle saddle horse or English hunter/jumper. I learned to ride and train all kinds on the ranch in El Monte."

One of the better horses Corpe had an interest in was a mare his father bred named No Butt. "She was the greatest quarter-racing horse that ever lived," said Corpe. "She still holds the world record for mares in a quarter-mile race. She was Horse of the Year in 1958, having won three world championship titles that year."

Ralph Corpe stayed with his father and brother-in-law, the great reinsman and racing trainer, Don "Pooch" Lieber, at the Sacramento ranch until 1968, when he was employed full-time by Mrs. William P. Roth to train her Western horses in Woodside, California. Corpe later started his own training facility in Woodside and worked for the late Nancy Burriss, millionairess of the Household Finance Company, among other equestrians.

He joined the staff of Coto de Caza in March of 1973 as head Western trainer both of horses and riders. Although he's qualified to teach English riding, Coto de Caza needed a Western man to fill in the staff under the direction of Max Bonham, director of the equestrian center, and staff trainer Bill Gobie, both of whom specialize in English training.

Ralph Corpe no longer has the time to school a horse from the ground up. "It's just more than I can do with all the commitments that need attention here at Coto de Caza," admits the man who trained Bobby Ingersoll, one of Northern California's greatest trainers. "I like to take a good horse that has had some basic training, such as one broken to the halter or saddle and doesn't have a lot of bad habits, then build from there.

"There are certain basic skills a horse must be able to accomplish to specialize in the show ring," he continues. "It doesn't take long to figure out if a particular animal will be good in a given class, or just make a pleasure horse for an individual or family."

Corpe's conformational criteria for an outstanding show prospect, regardless of the breed, are: width in the forehead between the eyes; nice, sharp, pretty ears; well-placed, expressive eyes; clean top line to his head; nice jaw; clean underline; small, refined muzzle; big, wide nostrils; long neck; a clean throat latch so that he shows good breeding facility; good slope to his shoulder; a short back with strong loin; length in the croup and hip; good, straight legs that come up to all four corners; a good tail set; depth through the heart; good barrel; solid, proportioned feet; and solid sloping pasterns.

"If he has all these attributes, you normally will have a really nice horse in any breed," notes the trainer of Curley Bill, a Pacific Coast champion jumper. "It doesn't make any difference if he's red, white and blue with purple polka dots—if he has the basic conformation, he'll in most cases be a good horse."

The trainer starts most of his horses as 2-year-olds and rides them lightly for a short time before turning them out to rest. "I then go back to training and begin showing them as 3-year-olds," adds Corpe. "Of course, there are exceptions; some I can start at 2 and go right on through to the show ring. These usually are the larger horses that are well fed and have the ability to go into "A" shows soon after the start of training. It depends on the breeding and a multitude of other factors, but, above all, you can't rush the training and come up with a good end result."

On the average, Corpe begins intensive training for Western classes, whether pleasure or performance, at about 2½ years of age. "We have to ride them pretty hard during this initial training, so they must be mature enough to stand the pressure," Corpe says. "If they're too young, you will get them tired and may injure the soft bones that still are developing."

He follows the three-month rule for Western training that is used by most Thoroughbred trainers. "You have to slow-gallop a young race horse at least three months before you set him down, or something—usually his legs—will give. The same holds true with Western training. The young, developing horse must build strength and stamina slowly and, although I recommend at least three months of light work before you can get down to hard work, some horses take even longer. If you rush it, there can be permanent injury, usually to the horse's legs. And, to use an old cliche, 'No legs, no horse'."

Ralph Corpe believes it's much easier to start the horse in a snaffle to teach it to turn, move forward in a straight line, and to keep the animal from bucking. A hackamore probably would hurt the horse's nose and might even ruin him for show or pleasure. "Go to a hackamore after you start him in a snaffle," he adds.

"The snaffle works on the corners of the horse's mouth, as opposed to the curb bit that puts pressure on the bars of the mouth, or the hackamore that applies pressure to the nose and jaw. If you jerk the horse around with the hackamore, the nose may become bruised and cut, and you'll end up with scar tissue that is insensitive and poor for showing. The curb bit can hurt the mouth, causing him to develop a hard mouth and be shy of bits later in life. So, as with most trainers, I firmly believe in starting the new horse in the snaffle."

If later on the owner wants Corpe to train the horse to show in a hackamore, he'll change over. Most amateur horsemen don't want or can't make the top shows with a hackamore horse, because of the expense in training, according to Ralph Corpe. "It can take a year or two—or even more—to train a great hackamore horse and most owners just can't or don't want to invest that kind of money," adds the man who trained Chap Stick, champion stock horse. "The majority of hackamore events in the big Western shows are taken by the professional trainers."

The saddle a trainer uses on a young horse is important both to the rider and horse. "I use a saddle that's been in my family for nearly forty years. I call it my colt saddle," Corpe states. "I use it when riding colts that are small around the girth, generally true of most colts I work with. I can cinch this saddle up good and tight, so it won't slide around and scare or injure the horse. Another reason is that, with a new horse, many times he'll roll over backwards and I don't want to ruin a good show saddle while training a young horse!"

Upon occasion, Corpe has used an English saddle during this initial schooling phase, particularly on horses too small for a Western saddle. "It's a strange thing that, when a colt bucks—and sometimes a green horse will, although I prefer not to let him—I can ride the jumping saddle better than the Western rig. My legs fit closer to the horse's barrel with the English saddle and I can get a better purchase on him. Too, you can feel the horse better.

"With the Western saddle, the cantle will hit my backside and I do a graceful flip over the horse's head, landing bottom-down, pulling the bridle off with me. The horse vanishes into the sunset and, after I get up, I have to chase the animal down. I can ride bucking horses, but that's a young man's sport and I'll leave it to them."

The length of time it takes to make a finished horse is, naturally, dependent upon the animal and the trainer. "I believe it takes two to three years to really train a horse well," he says. "Then again, the exceptions are numerous. My brother-in-law Pooch Lieber and I trained a horse called Miss Margo. She took the championship in her class at the California State Fair in Sacramento as a 3-year-old with only six weeks' training in the bridle and hackamore. Even more spectacular was a horse that Lieber trained named Grass Jr., that took reserve champion at the same fair at eighteen months of age, then won the championship the next two years!

"These horses were exceptions in both performance and attitude," he stresses. "Each animal reaches its pinnacle of ability at its own speed. There is no rule for time in training and, although you can tell if the horse will be able to do well in a certain show or performance event, the training time is impossible to predict."

The animal's sex may play an important part in the training of a horse. "Sex of the animal doesn't seem to make a great deal of difference, with the exception of stallions," Corpe says. "At one point in my career I trained one of my father's mares and I didn't then care for mares. I had had some bad-acting mares and was just down on them. As it turned out, this mare, called Oakley Annie, won the halter and reining championships at the California State Fair. She set what I believe was a distance record for the slide stop, seventy-six feet, in that show arena.

"Red Randall, who's a great trainer in Northern California, thinks mares or stallions are the best to train and doesn't care for any geldings. Here again, one of the greatest horses Red ever had was a champion gelding named Whirl Wind, an outstanding stock horse. It's pretty much a matter of personal taste with the individual trainer."

The exception is the stallion. There are valid reasons for gelding a stallion. "The stallions must be kept separate from other horses and, as a rule don't make good saddle horses for the average owner. Some studs, either before and especially after they've been bred, have a rotten disposition in public. On the other hand, a stallion I have in training called Foxy Mac, owned by Mrs. Jeanine Petrie of Mission Viejo, California, has a great disposition. He's smart, kind and just an exceptional horse.

"But by and large, the average horse owner is better off with a mare or gelding. Mares and geldings make good bridle horses, cutting horses, hunters and jumpers but, in most cases, we don't think of a stallion as a pleasure horse."

The first thing Corpe teaches his horses is "whoa," to kill the engine. "Whoa is the first thing you want to teach because if you get too much go and no whoa, you're in big trouble," he says.

"Anything you do on a horse is a forward motion, and getting a horse to go forward is no great problem," Foxy Mac's trainer adds. "Even if a horse is doing a spin, all he's doing is galloping in such a short circle that he actually pivots around a pivot foot. He's actually going forward so you always want to keep his hocks engaged and moving up under him. About two-thirds of the horse's weight should be carried on the back end, so he has to break at the poll.

"To spin a horse you lean into the turn with your weight over the pivot foot in the direction you are turning—using the opposite leg and spur. At the same time the reins direct his nose in the direction wanted.

"This is an example of a horse responding to pressure on his mouth," continues the horseman. "You want the animal to respond to light pressure from the fingers on the reins, but in actuality, most cues come from the legs and weight."

The trainer says there can be definite problems with a horse that's been trained only by using pressure on his mouth. "If you use only pressure on his mouth to stop and turn, the end product will be a limber-necked, unsteady horse that doesn't follow his head," he comments. "The hands control the front end and the legs control the back end. Both must be used to have an animal perform to his best ability."

After the animal has been taught to stop, Corpe then schools the horse in moving forward. "Don't be in a hurry and try not to let the animal buck," he advises. "The old-time breaking method of making a horse buck until he's tired is foolish, because you can eliminate this at the start by letting him know that he can't buck.

"Taking your time is important," he continues. "You teach him to walk, then jog slowly and do this in such a way that he's unafraid and relaxed. You must have his total attention during these phases, which is why I use a round corral with high walls. Also, this prevents a horse from running off; he can be turned into a wall and he'll stop."

The round corral at Coto de Caza is covered, the high walls cutting off most of the sights and sounds from outside. "To the horse, the round corral is a never-ending fence. You have his complete attention and he soon learns to relax. He will learn to canter and to take one lead, then the other. He quietly learns to perform properly and soon is ready for the big test, that of being let out in a large arena."

In the outside arena, with cars and other horses in sight, he still should perform properly, based on his previous isolated training. One occasionally may get bucked off but, as a rule, if one has prepared the horse well, he won't panic and will respond to what he's learned," says Corpe, who has trained several champion stock horses, including Woowie.

"From here, you can slowly repeat the earlier training, utilizing the large arena," Corpe comments. "When you feel the time is right, move into the open pasture and the trails. It's best if you are able to ride on a large piece of land, say, forty acres or more in size, so you can get the horse to relax while reinforcing the training you already have taught in the round corral and big arena."

As training the Western horse proceeds, Corpe also changes some of his tack. "If I'm not going to train a horse in a hackamore, I'll change to a bit and bridoon from the snaffle bit," he says. "This is a bit—usually a curb—and small English snaffle that's used in conjunction with a Western bosal so you have four reins with which to work. You can pick a horse's head up into a certain position with the snaffle and tuck his nose in with your curb bit. You have two hands to work so you work an indirect rein and a direct rein at all times to get a horse to follow his head and his nose. It works well in training the Western horse, although it's basically English equipment."

According to Corpe, if a trainer can get the horse's head where it's wanted, one is in good shape. "Many people say it's the mouth; does a horse have a good mouth? I always say it's reaching the brain. It's the brain that responds to leg, weight and voice aids, not the mouth."

Depending upon the event for which the horse is being trained, after he's mastered the basics Corpe starts honing the horse's skills to perfection. This leads to one of the toughest questions a trainer must answer: How many hours each week will he ride a customer's horse while in training?

"There is no rule of thumb as to time each day for a week I'll ride a horse while in training," answers Corpe. "Each animal learns at his own pace. I teach horses for an hour or more each day. This may vary where one horse needs only forty-five minutes of work, and the next may take an hour and a half. A parallel may be that of the public school system, where each student varies in his or her ability to learn at a given pace. There is no set time schedule for training horses or people."

A horse destined to work in "A" or "B" shows shouldn't be worked too much each day. "If you ride him for two or three hours each training session, he will be too fit for the show arena," stresses the trainer. "It will take several hours of riding to wear him down so he'll look relaxed and not nervous at the show when away from home.

"I've had horses so trained-up that, when we would go to a show, they would break out in a sweat and be so nervous that they just looked terrible," continues Corpe. "You wouldn't be able to take him into the show ring. One horse I had to ride all day, switching off with the owner, to get him tired enough to be calm and look good during the show."

Corpe tries to get the horse in training and the owner or rider together as soon as possible, but this is another "iffy" situation. "If the rider is experienced, knows how to ride in perfect balance, has good hands, good timing and coordination, then you can start the rider as soon as the horse is trained to the point that the rider won't get hurt. That's why I get paid for hard knocks.

"If you have a green rider and a green horse, you must take your time in marrying up the rider with the horse or you'll ruin all the training that's been taught to the animal," continues Corpe, trainer of Carol Vicini, who was undefeated as a junior for two years when with Corpe. "It's far better to start the inexperienced rider on another well-trained horse, because the inexperienced rider wants to do too much before he's ready to perform well.

"It's a matter of judgment. When I see that both the horse and the rider are ready, I then will put them together. It's just a hard fact of life that the rider must be patient and learn before he can ride properly. He's still going to make mistakes, but he won't ruin the training I've worked on and he's paid for. It's good if you can watch the owner riding his horse and correct him as he rides his own animal. Hopefully, he will get the proper feel of riding in a short time."

Ralph Corpe relates one of his biggest problems: "It's when you get a horse going along to a certain point and the inexperienced rider says, 'That's all I can afford,' then takes the animal home. Within a week, he's ruined everything I have done. Then he'll blame the trainer and not his own inexperience. There's an old saying that I heard as a youngster and it's still true: 'If you don't wait on a horse, it makes you wait.' "

Is any breed easier to train than another? "Definitely," he observes. "There are many breeds that are just not adapted mentally or physically to become a top Western show horse. There always are execeptions to this rule, but by and large the quarter horse has been the top Western horse in the world.

"One must remember that the quarter horse actually was bred for Western work and it should stand to reason that he would do well at Western showing," continues the trainer of Premium Chex, another Corpe-trained champion stock horse. "It's not fair to knock any breed, because there are some outstanding individual Western show horses from most of the other registries. But in my book, the quarter horse is the star when it comes to Western showing."

The trainer stresses that the learning process never stops. "Whenever you're riding a horse, you are training him, whether you're a professional trainer or not," he says. "Anyone can ruin a good horse by riding him the wrong way, so remember this always."

The trainer says that, even with his years of experience with horses, he's still learning. "Anybody who tells you he knows everything about training horses either is a liar or just plain stupid," he comments. "Each time I get on a new horse, I say 'show me,' because you don't always go the same route with every single horse. You may have to change completely your training criteria with one horse, as opposed to the one you just finished."

Corpe also maintains that a horse, at some point during his training, will test the trainer. "They all give you a battle during training at one time or another," he says. "It may take a long time in coming, but it will come and you'd better win your battle. If you don't, the horse will go his own way.

"Many people make the tragic mistake of buying a green horse for a green rider. They ride the animal before they buy him and he goes pretty well. You get the horse home and the first thing you know, he bucks off your daughter. She goes back and says, 'He didn't mean it,' then gives him a carrot, gets on and he bucks her off again. The horse has won the battle and he is going to do what he wants.

"You as parents are saying, 'Well, that so-and-so who sold us this rank horse ought to be locked up.' It's your fault, not the seller's. You don't expect a teen-age teacher to teach your teen-ager in high school, so how can you expect an inexperienced young horse to understand or obey the direction of an inexperienced young rider?"

As stated, California is one of the country's best training grounds of good horses. There can be no doubt this is, to a degree, due to the efforts of those trainers like Ralph Corpe.

PREFACE TO SECTIONS II AND III

Perhaps one of the attractions of the horse is that he presents a challenge on so many levels. Master one discipline, and there are still a dozen more to be learned; compete successfully in one class, and there is always a more advanced one to follow. No matter what your degree of proficiency, there are always more worlds to conquer, new fields to explore.

In recent years, many adventurous horsemen have abandoned the traditional show ring to take part in more strenuous forms of competition. The worlds they seek to conquer are those of Long-Distance Riding and Combined Training. In the next two sections, top professionals in both fields will tell you what they're all about and how and where you can compete—if you have the spirit and the stamina.

SECTION II

LONG-DISTANCE RIDING

Long-Distance Riding

By
HEATHER SMITH THOMAS

Long-distance contesting is not for the weekend pleasure rider.

Covering long distances on horseback, at one time a necessity, has been turned into a sport in the form of endurance and competitive trail riding. But before taking up this pastime, make sure you and your horse are ready for it.

This kind of sport is not for the weekend pleasure rider or the horseman who likes a sleek, fat animal that can stand around in a show ring for 20 minutes. It is only for the horseman who likes to work with his horse every day, enjoys long hours in the saddle and prides himself in having a good horse that is sound, healthy and able to stay that way under rigorous conditions. A long-distance horse has to have the go power and staying ability to undertake strenuous work with ease, and the long-distance rider must be determined and durable, and horseman enough to condition his horse properly and get the most from him.

There have been many outstanding long-distance rides throughout history that have resulted in amazing records of endurance. Some of these were planned rides, while others were made during war in valiant attempts to get help or send messages. The U.S. Cavalry conditioned its horses for long marches (sometimes a unit had to be able to travel 250-300 miles in a week) and held its own endurance contests for the best horses and riders.

The leader of modern day endurance rides is the annual Tevis Cup ride, which began as the Western States 100-Mile-One Day Ride in 1955 to prove a point. Many horsemen felt that modern horses were not as tough as those in the past. Wendell Robie, an Arabian horse breeder, disagreed and argued the point with a friend. He volunteered to try to ride 100 miles in 24 hours or less.

The route Robie chose was from Lake Tahoe across the old Sierra Nevada Pony Express route to Auburn, California. It covered all kinds of terrain and had a good variation in elevation (Tahoe City is 6,000 feet, Emmigrant Pass is 7,930 feet, and Auburn is only 1,000 feet). Robie was sure he could make the ride, and to make the test even more conclusive he talked four other men into going with him.

Four of the five riders made the 100 miles in less than 24 hours. Enthusiastic friends and well-wishers thought these men had done the impossible, and they wanted to try it, too. So the next year, the 100-mile ride was born and became an annual event. Since then, all who compete in the ride receive a silver and gold belt buckle for their achievement.

In 1959, Will Tevis, who held several endurance records himself, and his brothers donated the silver Tevis Cup that goes to the person each year who makes the fastest time with his horse in good condition. And in 1964, Louis Haggin donated the James B. Haggin Cup, honoring his great-grandfather who was a noted racehorse breeder, which is presented each year to the horse among the first 10 finishers that makes the ride in best condition.

Endurance vs. competitive riding; there is a difference.

The Tevis Cup has helped pave the way for today's long-distance endurance and competitive trail riding contests. Although both the endurance ride and competitive trail ride are contests that are long-distance rides, and both require horses to be in good condition for travelling long distances in a short time, that's where the similarity ends.

The endurance ride is a race. The rider who gets his horse from start to finish in the shortest time while maintaining his horse's physical condition is the winner. The competitive trail ride is not a race, but the rider must usually complete the ride within a specified time. Judging in a competitive trail ride often places some emphasis on good horsemanship, well-trained and well-mannered horses, as well as soundness and condition. There is usually a point system that takes condition, time and those other factors in consideration to decide the winner.

The North American Trail Ride Conference (NATRC) has many rides throughout the country that are all staged and judged under a strict set of rules. Participants can accumulate points in these rides from their various weight divisions (heavyweight, lightweight and junior) for end-of-the-year awards.

Endurance rides have always been an individual thing, but in 1971 the American Endurance Ride Conference was established to standardize rules, establish nonconflicting dates and help provide information about endurance riding.

There are some differences between NATRC contests and endurance rides. NATRC rides have a minimum and maximum time limit, so a rider who comes in too early or too late is penalized. Endurance rides have no minimum time limit and a rider is disqualified only if he takes longer than the maximum time.

NATRC rides are judged on condition of horse (40 percent), soundness (40 percent), manners and way of going (20 percent), and there are usually awards for horsemanship, also. Endurance rides are judged on speed, soundness, condition and ability of the horse to proceed. Manners and way of going aren't counted and a horse is not disqualified on manners unless he interferes with other horses on the trail or is too nasty to let the veterinarians examine him.

In both endurance and NATRC rides there are check points along the trail where the horse's condition is checked by veterinarians for temperature, pulse and respiration (TPR) and for lameness, though some NATRC rides only check for pulse and respiration. Rules of both events are to protect the horse, and any

Long-distance competitive riding covers rugged territory and tests the endurance of horse and rider. This group of trail riders goes up a ridge in the Salmon River areas of Idaho on a long-distance ride.

horse that is not fit to continue will be pulled.

An endurance ride is generally longer than a competitive trail ride. It's a contest in which the same horse and rider cover a set course, usually 50-100 miles, with the first horse to finish in acceptable condition being the winner. There are no weight divisions, but usually all horses must carry a minimum weight of 150 pounds, including rider, saddle and tack. At the end of the year the AERC selects a national champion endurance horse and rider from points earned during competition on a one-horse, one-rider basis.

If the first horse to cross the finish line in an endurance ride is in no condition to continue on, he will not be the winner. This rule protects the horse from an overly-eager rider who might use him up to be first across the finish line. Occasionally this happens and the first horse is not declared winner if the veterinarians feel he was used up excessively or came through in an unsound condition.

There are some competitive trail rides that are neither endurance rides nor NATRC contests. The Rocky Mountain Competitive Trail Ride Association, with rides in Montana, Idaho, Wyoming and Canada, has contests from 30-60 miles which combine some of the characteristics of endurance and competitive trail riding. These rides are not races, but do have terrain and times similar to endurance rides. They offer advantages of both endurance and competitive trail riding.

Good horse needed for serious riding.

If you plan to compete seriously in long-distance riding, you need a good horse. Almost any kind of horse, as long as he is sound, will

Mrs. Thomas gets her endurance horses in condition by working cattle on their ranch. The horses may be ridden 2,500 miles a year doing ranch work.

do on some of the shorter rides with good training and conditioning. But if the longer, tougher rides are your goal, take care in selecting your mount.

Choose one that's at least five or six years old. You won't be so apt to injure him with hard work and he'll hold up better under stress. Choose a horse with good conformation—sloping shoulders and pasterns, correct feet and legs. A horse with good conformation and a straight way of travelling will hold up better than the poorly conformed horse. He'll have better "shock absorbers" in his pasterns and won't likely go lame or unsound with strenuous, steady work. The horse with a good slope in his shoulders and pasterns will have a freer, smoother gait for better traveling, and you'll get a more comfortable ride. A horse with jarring gaits is hard on himself and you. The concussion will cause leg problems sooner or later.

Pay close attention to how the horse travels, because any tendency to interfere or forge will become more pronounced when he is tired. A horse may strike himself towards the end of a long ride, even though he doesn't normally interfere when he is fresh.

Look hard at the Arabians and part-Arabians for serious competition. These little horses have the heart, stamina and weight-carrying ability for long, strenuous rides. The Arabian is one breed that seems to dominate the winner's circle in endurance riding. A big, stout type of horse has advantages in heavy roping or other events where size, weight and strength count, but on the long trail a little horse has an advantage over the larger animal and a light-muscled horse has the advantage over the heavily muscled one.

A big horse has a lot of weight to pack around. All that muscle may be great for a quick sprint, but it can be burdensome on a 50- or 100-mile ride. Exertion produces energy and waste products. Thc conversion to energy and elimination of wastes in the muscles is more efficient in the lighter-muscled horse. By-products of energy production accumulate rapidly in the muscles during exertion and must be carried away in the blood stream. This process is slower in the heavy-muscled horse. Azoturia and "tying up" occur more often in the heavier horse, while the small, light-muscled horse is less likely to have this metabolic problem.

The smaller horse, like the Arabian with his short, strong back, has more weight-carrying ability for his size than does the big horse. Winners of the tough endurance rides over the years include a lot of small, 750-to-900-pound Arabians carrying big men. So don't underestimate the small horse when choosing an endurance prospect.

In my opinion, heart and willingness count for almost as much in determining the stamina of a horse as does conformation and soundness. Of course, you want a horse that is sound and looks good, but he also has to have drive and willingness to make a top long-distance horse. If there is a choice between a horse with perfect conformation and one not-so-perfect but with guts and willpower, pick the latter if you can condition him carefully and keep him sound. A horse must *want* to go to compete successfully on a long ride. If he is lazy and you have to urge him every step of the way, he won't get far and you'll be beat before you start. You want a horse that travels willingly and easily on his own. This is another reason the hot-blooded horse is a natural for long-distance riding. He gets "fired up" and eager and wants to go the whole distance.

Conditioning takes time and work.

Start early to condition a horse for an endurance or competitive trail ride, preferably several months before the event. If the horse is soft when you begin, work slow and gradual because a soft horse is more likely to become overworked or injured than one whose tendons and muscles are in good shape.

Start with short rides and the walk, gradually legging up the horse and strengthening his muscles. Then add longer rides with more trotting, and finally some galloping to build up his wind as he begins to get in shape. As the horse becomes harder, do a lot of trotting, for this is the most important gait for the long-distance horse. You want to develop it to its fullest. The trot is a well-balanced gait and best for maintaining good speed over long periods of time without the horse becoming overly tired. Work on the trot until your horse moves freely, easily and willingly.

Early in the conditioning program, you should have your horse wormed and his teeth checked. He'll do a better job of utilizing his feed and get in shape faster (and stay that way) if he is not host to a heavy infestation of internal parasites or doesn't have trouble eating. Internal parasites use a lot of nutrients and can sap a horse's reserve energy. If you're going to demand a great deal from a horse, give him half a chance with a good worming program early in his conditioning, and KEEP him wormed.

What you feed is important as you try to build up your horse's energy and endurance. He should have an adequate and well-balanced diet, with amounts increased gradually as his work increases. If he is on good pasture, he may only need a daily grain ration during the early stages of conditioning. As he gets farther along and the work is harder and longer, add some hay to his diet.

Most irrigated pasture grasses contain too much water for the amount of nutrients they provide, and are a "soft" feed. He can get more nutrition per volume in dry feeds. Select the best quality hay you can find. You may want to use a vitamin and mineral supplement as well, and make sure he always has access to salt.

The amount and type of grain you feed will depend on your own preferences and on the individual horse. Some horses need more grain than others. When feeding grain, remember to cut down the amount on days the horse doesn't work. And on days you ride, feed the grain ration well before you start to ride. Don't give a horse a lot of feed and then work him hard. Give him at least an hour or two to digest it.

As you begin conditioning the horse, let your veterinarian check him for health and soundness. A blood count is a good idea if you want to get your horse in top shape. This will show the horse's condition and detect any anemia. If his blood count is low, vitamins and injections can correct the problem. Red blood cells transport fresh supplies of oxygen to the muscles and also remove the waste products. A blood count taken at the beginning of your conditioning program and another later, as your horse gets into shape, will tell how the horse is doing and will give you time to work out any problems.

Check the color of your horse's gums and the inside of his nostrils. If they are a healthy pink, he probably is not anemic and his blood is in good shape. If they are white, you have a problem because lack of color in gums and nostrils usually means a low blood count or overwork.

The real test of your ability to condition a horse is in your judgment of how much stress to give the horse. Build him up gradually, but stress him so that he becomes able to do more and more work. Don't overdo him, yet challenge him. Stress him a bit so that he continually develops his muscles, wind and "reserve"—the ability to go a little farther.

You condition your horse along a fine line, and you need an intimate feel of how much your horse can take without souring. You must know his abilities and potential and be able to tell how he is progressing. You must judge how much more he should be able to do this week than last week, without hurting him or discouraging him. To help, don't do the same old thing on the same trail day after day. Give your horse variety by changing the routine, traveling different country and taking on new and different obstacles.

After the horse is legged up and getting in shape, part of his conditioning can be workouts at the gallop to build up his wind. But the main aid in conditioning your horse will be the 10-to-30-mile hike, a lot of it at the trot. And climb some good hills. A two-mile gallop on days you don't take the long ride will help keep him in shape, but it's a poor substitute for miles on the trail.

Avoid over-conditioning your horse. If you are preparing for a 50-mile ride, DON'T ride him that far every day. Take him out for 25-35 miles, perhaps two or three times a week, with shorter rides, gallops or days of rest in between. And you don't need your long rides to be in winning time. Shoot for a maximum effort the day of the ride, so don't use up your horse before the ride. You want to peak your horse on the day of the ride. He should be coming along well and built up so he can give his maximum effort that day. He shouldn't be leg-weary and discouraged.

Learn how to take your horse's temperature, pulse and respiration (TPR). He'll have to be used to this so he won't object to being handled by the veterinarians and TPR crews while in competition. And a knowledge of his pulse, respiration and temperature can help in his conditioning, so you can tell how he's coming along.

Respiration rate can easily be counted by watching the horse's nostrils or flanks. Instead of counting for a minute, count the breaths for 15 seconds and multiply by four for a fairly accurate count. Pulse can be taken with a stethoscope at the horse's girth, or felt with the fingers at the jaw, root of the tail or pastern area just above the heel bulbs. Temperature is taken rectally, but tie a string to the end of the thermometer so you won't lose it. Find out

Long walks and trots really get the horse in shape. After a long ride, always cool your horse out.

what your horse's TPR rates are when he's at rest, and then take readings when he is stressed to see how high they go. Then take them 10 minutes later to find how much they return to normal after a short rest.

Heart rate at rest in a healthy horse can vary from about 36 to 50 beats a minute, with 40 being about average. Respiration at rest is from 8 to 24, with 16 being average. Normal temperature in a horse can vary from 99 to 100.5 degrees.

When a horse is working hard, all these rates go up. If he is stressed hard, respiration may go up to 90; temperature may climb to 102 or 103, and pulse rate may go up as high as 120. But if he is in good condition, these rates should begin to drop as soon as he stops to rest (a horse in top-notch shape probably won't have rates quite this high) and should be down to nearly normal within 10 minutes. As you condition your horse you'll notice it takes him less and less time to cool out after a workout and his rates will drop down to normal fairly quickly.

If a horse's pulse or respiration does not drop markedly, or if they increase after a 10-minute rest period, you are stressing him too much. He's not ready to take it. In any horse, if the respiration rate becomes faster than the pulse (where he's panting and breathing rapidly and shallowly), he has reached the point of exhaustion and his health is in danger. If he is pushed beyond this point, his temperature will suddenly drop into subnormal ranges and he may go into shock.

When a horse is in good condition, his TPRs will return to normal quickly after exertion. This recovery rate is what the TPR crew and veterinarians check for during a competitive trail ride. What the horse's readings are when you arrive at a check point are not nearly as important as how much the rates drop and come to normal within the rest period.

Rest your horse whenever you think he needs it during a long ride. If you get off, loosen the cinch for a few minutes to let him breathe easier. Lift the saddle a bit to let air circulate under the pad and cool his back, and let him catch his breath. On a long ride, it is all right to let the horse drink when he is thirsty, as long as he doesn't drink too much and he keeps moving afterward. It refreshes him and then he won't try to tank up all at once when he gets hot and dry. It's not good to let a hot horse drink a lot of cold water at once, especially if he will be standing around afterwards. Cold water sends blood rushing to the stomach, leaving the stressed muscles in a lurch, and can cause severe colic, or even founder.

Proper riding can help your horse.

You can help your horse in competition by riding properly and using the right equipment. A good long-distance rider is out of his saddle more than he is in it. He rides on his feet and balanced with his weight forward, never pounding down on the horse's back or riding on his loins.

You have to condition yourself as well as the horse so you can make a long ride without tiring. Don't have someone else condition your horse and then expect to ride that horse well in competition. YOU have to be in shape, too.

Never sag or slouch in the saddle. Keep your weight balanced up where the horse can carry it best. A tired rider makes a tired horse, creating a drag on him and possibly hurting the horse's kidneys or making his back sore. Keep your weight forward when going up and down steep hills. He can carry it with less effort and you'll not hinder his loins and hind quarters. Keep him collected in rough country, especially going down hill, with his hind feet well under himself. He'll be more surefooted.

Make sure your saddle fits the horse properly. Ill-fitting equipment will do if you don't ride often, but the daily work in conditioning for long-distance riding can make a lot of sore spots if your gear doesn't fit or isn't kept clean. Make sure your tack fits. Use a saddle pad that is thick and soft, preferably one you can wash often. Keep it very clean, and your horse clean and well-groomed, too.

While in long-distance competition, your horse should be able to mind his manners at all times. He should be able to tolerate handling by TPR crews, which is considered in scoring competitive trail rides.

You may want to use light equipment. If the ride has weight divisions, being in the lighter divisions is best. And your tack is dead weight, so you want to make the horse's load as light as possible. This is why many endurance riders use flat saddles or McClellans. On a long ride, every pound counts.

Pay special attention to your horse's feet as you condition him. Keep him properly trimmed and shod. He shouldn't have hoof cracks, thrush or brittle or soft feet. If he is kept in a corral or soft pasture, take him out in the rocks and break him in gradually. He needs his feet toughened up before tackling a trail ride, because there is usually rocky terrain to cover. Hoof pads are used on a lot of horses on many endurance rides to protect their feet from excessive bruising. But some trail rides won't permit them. If you live in a dry climate you may need a hoof dressing or conditioner to keep your horse's feet from getting dry or brittle.

Plan your shoeing program well, because the shoes can mean the difference between success and failure on a long ride. If your horse's feet aren't in good shape or are poorly shod, he may go lame. He should be shod every 6-8 weeks, depending on his rate of hoof growth. If he wears shoes out more often than this, apply some hard-surface material, such as borium, on the ground surface of the shoes to make them last longer. Also, if shoes are put on too often, your horse will run out of hoof room for new nails.

The last set of shoes put on your horse before a ride should definitely be hard-surfaced, and be applied about three or four weeks prior to competition. You'll want your farrier to leave plenty of hoof and sole for the ride because your horse may have lots of rocky ground to cover. If his feet have been recently trimmed and shod, he may get bruised and tender more easily.

Later, in conditioning your horse, speed up his trot and learn to post. Posting is easier on you and the horse and keeps you better balanced over his back. I like to post low, carrying my weight almost entirely in my stirrups and legs, rising a little from the saddle each time and never really sitting down.

After a long time in the saddle, be careful how you take that saddle off. There has been a lot of pressure on the horse's back and the blood is somewhat depressed from the area. If you get off suddenly and take the saddle off, this pressure is released all at once and blood rushes back. This can sometimes cause permanent lumps and bumps on his back. If you've been on a long ride, get off and lead the horse a little before taking the saddle off. Loosen the cinch and lift the saddle a time or two to let air under it, then take it off.

Your horse should mind his manners.

You should work on your horse's manners as well as his physical condition during the training program. Accustom him to new things so he'll be prepared in actual competition. If you'll have to haul him there, get him trailer trained. If the contest is a competitive trail ride, remember that he'll be judged on manners as well as condition, so spend time getting him used to thorough handling. He shouldn't kick at a TPR girl or bite a judge.

Teach him to stand still and to tolerate people walking around him, touching him and picking up his feet. At check points the TPR crews will put a stethoscope at his girth and a thermometer in his rectum. The horse should stand quietly with no fuss. The vet will feel his back and other places to check for soreness or swelling. If any of this handling bothers your horse, work on him before the ride so he'll stand and take it.

Get your horse accustomed to being around other horses and working alone as well. He should travel alone without fussing, and not pay attention to other horses that pass him or that he passes.

He should be used to being in a stall or tied up all night. On some rides, horses are stabled in stalls the night before and after the ride. They may be tied up on other rides. He should be ready for this, and be able to rest the night before without fretting because of strange conditions.

If your horse will have to be tied, tie him up all night at home a few times before the ride. Tie him to a trailer or tree and give him feed and water there. Give him barely enough rope to reach the ground to eat, drink and even lie down. On the ride, you can bring along some straw for bedding where you tie him. And sleep close by so you can help if he gets in trouble.

When is a horse ready for a 100-mile ride? This is answered in terms of his conditioning, when he has reached the point where he can travel for long periods of time at good trotting speed without getting very tired. After a short rest, his recovery rate is good and he is then able and willing to go on.

If your horse is ready, are you ready? Can you measure your horse's capabilities without hurting him. The rider who uses good judgment will do a better job. He has to be able to sense his horse's fatigue and give him rest or slower work when needed. A rider who is tired himself may fail to judge his horse accurately and may run out of horse. Good seat, good hands and good balance will help keep you from tiring so you can help your horse.

How much can you ask of your horse? On a long ride you must constantly feel for your horse's capabilities as you go along. Use judgement so you won't overuse your horse on certain parts of the trail and not have enough saved for later. Learning to pace is also important, and experience is the best way to learn.

On a long ride, you'll learn more about your horse in one day than you might learn in a whole lifetime of ordinary riding. Endurance riding takes a special kind of rider with a special way of thinking when it comes to using his horse, because the endurance horse works a lot harder than the average horse.

A Comparison Between Endurance Riding and Competitive Trail Riding

By
RICHARD B. BARSALEAU, D.V.M.
and
SHARON SAARE

During the past 15 years, the sports of endurance riding and competitive trail riding have shown a marked increase in popularity. With the founding of the Western States Trail Ride, Inc. (Tevis Cup), in the middle 1950's and the establishment of the North American Trail Ride Conference (NATRC) in 1961, we have seen the two philosophies of competition gain their own enthusiastic followers. Not only that, many riders embrace both fields of competition using the same horse for both.

This being so, why is there so much confusion as to the difference between a pure endurance ride event and the competitive trail ride? Both of these events have many things in common, including the philosophy of properly using a horse on the trail within his capacity, and demonstrating his ability to withstand the stresses of competition.

If we list a number of the areas of evaluation and control, we might best clarify the two types of rides. The assessment that follows should show how the two forms of trail riding are alike and how they are different.

	ENDURANCE RIDING	COMPETITIVE TRAIL RIDING
Objectives	To demonstrate the enduring qualities of horses (and riders) while being used over extended distances of trail (50 to 102 miles) within a maximum time limit; but ordinarily not requiring a minimum time limit.	To stimulate interest in the breeding and use of good trail horses possessed of stamina, soundness, and hardiness. To learn and demonstrate proper methods of training and conditioning horses for competitive riding. To encourage horsemanship in competitive trail riding. To demonstrate care and good usage of horses during and after rides without artificial methods or stimulants.
Judging of Horses	Areas of systemic locomotor, attitudinal, and body lesion evaluation are made. Horse is to remain serviceably sound and must show reasonable recovery values in pulse and respiration rates. He must show ability and willingness to move on; present few if any body lesions due to poorly fitted tack. Way of going is not considered except as it relates to locomotor soundness. Manners not considered unless horse is dangerous to examining officials or other horses and riders on the trail.	Areas of: Condition—40% Soundness—40% Manners—15% Way of going—5%
Theory of Judging	Allow horses in acceptable condition to proceed on the trail. Abide by the ride rules and see that they are followed by riders also. Only licensed veterinarians serve the rides as judges. (Preferably equine practitioners or horse-oriented veterinarians.)	All horses are to complete the designated trail ride in approximately the same time, with the veterinary judges evaluating the horse based on condition, soundness, manners, and way of going. Deficit points are subtracted from the total possible score of 100 points. Licensed veterinarians serve the ride as well as lay horsemanship judges. Decisions are based on agreement of both judges.
Veterinary Judge Control	Complete control in areas of decision regarding condition of the horses.	Complete control in areas of decision regarding condition of horses. Responsible for scoring horses according to NATRC rules.
Entry Fees	Variable, depending on ride management. Most 100-miles-in-one-day rides are presently requiring a $50-$60 entry fee.	Variable but usually of modest amount—$15 to $20 plus cost of meals.

	ENDURANCE RIDING	COMPETITIVE TRAIL RIDING
Age of Horse	Must be 5 years of age or older.	Novice Rides—may use 4-year-olds. Open Divisions—must be 5 or older.
Distance of Rides	Usually 50-102 miles in one day.	In Class A Rides, 25-40 miles daily for two consecutive days. In Class B Rides, one day of 25-40 miles.
Weight of Rider	Varied rules: most rides require 150-lb. minimum (tack and rider).	Heavyweight Division—rider and tack over 190 lbs. Lightweight Division—rider and tack between 140-189 lbs. Junior Division—no weight limit.
Timing	Mostly open-ended with a maximum time only. Minimum time on one cash-awarded ride where condition is scored most heavily, determining winner.	Both maximum and minimum times with 6½ to 7 hours riding time per day.
Speed	Depending on distance of ride, may average 5-15 m.p.h.	The average is between 4-7 m.p.h depending on the terrain.
Pulse and Respiration Parameters	The recovery time and rates of these two parameters are used to determine degree of condition; may aid in judge's decision to allow horses to continue on ride.	The recovery time and rates for pulse and respiration are used as part of criteria for determining horse's condition.
Dead Weight Allowed?	Yes, to make minimum-weight rule enforceable.	Yes, to make minimum-weight rule enforceable.
Rider Allowed Afoot?	Yes, may advance on trail either mounted or dismounted.	No. Rider *must be mounted* to advance on trail in order to maintain standardization of judging.
Drugging	Not allowed. Care should be taken to insure that a prohibited drug is not administered either by injection or by local (topical) application.	Not Allowed. Same precaution recommended here.
Grooming Assistants	Allowable. May be used to feed, groom, and care for horses at rest stops and at conclusion of ride.	None allowed. Rider will groom and care for his own horse.

ENDURANCE RIDING	COMPETITIVE TRAIL RIDING
Junior Division	
Not specified; however juniors may be *required* to ride with an adult sponsor.	Specified division . . . riders between 10-17 years. Juniors ride over same trail as open division riders, unaccompanied by sponsors or adults.
Progress on Final Two Miles of Trail	
Not controlled by speed nor manner of rating speed.	Horse must maintain forward motion in a most direct route following the marked trail.
Shoeing and Padding of Feet	
Not restricted insofar as types of shoes or pads.	No pads allowed to cover sole or frog.
Night Care of Horses	
No restrictions.	In keeping with uniformity requirements, no handling after 10 p.m. except in emergencies. To insure the horses' well being, a stable steward keeps them under observation.
Morning After Ride Care	
No restrictions.	No handling (other than feeding and watering) until the morning judging is completed.
Status Restrictions	
Pregnant mares are prohibited on all 100-miles-in-one-day rides.	None defined.
Novice Division	
No provision for novice horses or novice riders.	Used routinely for working young horses more moderately; introductory method to competitive trail riding, instructional value, shortened and less stressful courses, etc.
Racing Aspects of Competition	
Although many participants are primarily interested in completion awards, there is a definite racing aspect to endurance riding due to its open-ended timing factor. The true responsibility for the welfare of the horse rests with the rider; however, to insure that in the heat of competition the rider's enthusiasm does not exceed his judgment, the race should be controlled by the veterinary judges to prevent damage to horseflesh.	None encouraged and no advantage since the time factor controls the pace of NATRC rides.

ENDURANCE RIDING	COMPETITIVE TRAIL RIDING
Horsemanship	
Neither awarded nor considered . . . except in cases in which the condition of the horse warrants elimination (cruelty, abuse, etc.).	Evaluated by a horsemanship judge and scored in areas of grooming, handling, trail and stable care of horse, trail courtesy, tack and equipment care. Emphasis is given to proper equitation as it applies to trail riding.
Ride Secretary (Recorder)	
Routinely utilized and is a valuable person for record-keeping.	Designated by ride management; responsible for all records of judges, horsemanship judges, etc.
Ride Steward	
None designated. A ride officer may implement management policy if so designated.	Must be an approved NATRC member and must be familiar with all NATRC rules. A *required* duty on all NATRC rides.
Awards	
1) Completion awards: buckles, cups, medallions, silver plates, etc. are given to all horses finishing in satisfactory condition within the maximum time limits. 2) First horse in . . . usually special trophy award, occasionally cash and equipment awards, etc. 3) Best-condition award . . . selected usually from top ten finishers. 4) Breed awards: first finishing registered horse of each breed.	Individual rides: Open 1) Completion points to all who finish ride. Points added to annual scoring total. 2) Horse: heavyweight, lightweight, and junior; 1st-6th receive trophy and ribbons. 3) Sweepstakes: high-point horse from heavyweight, lightweight, and junior divisions. 4) Breed awards to high-point registered horse of each breed. 5) Horsemanship: junior & senior awards . . . 1-6th. 6) Novice awards: same as open. Annual Awards: 1) National sweepstakes champion. Highest points from the heavyweight, lightweight, and junior divisions. 2) National and regional championships based on placings and/or points within entire association activities and in restricted regional activities.
Value of Competition	
Endurance riding is discipline both for horse and rider. Teaches restraint, moderation in human behavior, compassion for the horse, the value of constant assessment of both oneself and one's horse, spartan training methods, and	Competitive trail riding is discipline both for horse and rider. Teaches value of basic horsemanship, appreciation and compassion for the horse, value of constant assessment of both oneself and one's horse, regular riding habits,

ENDURANCE RIDING	COMPETITIVE TRAIL RIDING
appreciation of good horseflesh. This sport determines who has done his "homework" insofar as preparation is concerned.	and appreciation of the finer points in good horsemanship. Teaches one to evaluate a good trail horse. Winning is determined by consistent effort in making a successful "team" of horse and rider during the event.

There you have some of the commonly described aspects of both types of competition. As you can readily see, to be successful in either field, you have to put a good deal of thought and time in the making of your trail horse. Selection of the horse, by itself, is very important if you plan to campaign for the top placings.

The day-to-day work schedule must be planned with the horse's basic conditioning program in mind *plus* a continual evaluation of just how the team is working out.

One should be aware that the endurance horse that is aiming for the top ten finishing group must possess a greater degree of stamina and condition than the horse who will only be expected to complete the course within the maximum time limits. Also, we should expect the top competitive horse to demonstrate an above average amount of training, savvy, and manners.

Both endurance riding and competitive trail riding are here to stay! They will keep ride management and veterinary judges busy just keeping up with them as enthusiasm grows from coast to coast!

See you on the trails! And bring along your good trail horse!

Why Five?

By
BILL THROGMORTON, D.V.M
and SHARON SAARE

"The Appaloosa Horse Club, Inc. has included distance riding, both competitive and endurance, in its Medallion Award System. Besides the many benefits to the rider who hits the distance trail, ApHC feels that one of the greatest values of distance riding to the light horse industry is as a test of soundness and durability. For the reasons set forth within this article, ApHC limits participation in its endurance and competitive programs to horses five or older."

SHARON SAARE
Director of Distance Riding
Appaloosa Horse Club, Inc.

"As a practicing veterinarian, I am asked every day to examine and judge the soundness of horses. It is apparent to me that those horses that receive too much work too young have the highest incidence of unsoundness. In thirteen years of judging trail riding horses, I have time and again seen the damage resulting from too much work too soon . . . and at the same time, have observed horses that went into distance riding at maturity and were successfully campaigned for several years."

BILL THROGMORTON, D.V.M.
Endurance and Competitive Ride Judge
Member, Judges Committee, American Association of Equine Practitioners

"Why five?" is asked by competitive and endurance trail ride enthusiasts every day. Why not ride three- or four-year-olds? Although the answer is evident, some riders would prefer to sidestep the facts and go along with economics and convenience.

The economics of horse raising today puts

considerable pressure on the owner to use young horses. Its costs around $300 a year minimum to feed a horse. Holding a horse for two years (between three and five) makes an additional cost of $600 without apparent direct benefit.

Not only are there feeding costs involved, but there are housing and other care costs. These costs will fluctuate from year to year and will differ in various areas, being much higher in some. But, regardless of the details, the principle is the same—it costs money to grow a horse to maturity and the expense involved prompts some people to want to use young horses before they are physically ready to compete.

Another factor is that many individuals today who are raising horses operate on a relatively small scale and become very personally involved with their stock. Because each horse is one of the family, they are anxious to see their product do well; make a name for his line, and the sooner the better.

In addition, they have often heard that a horse must have exercise early in life to properly develop heart and lung capacity. This theory has much merit and is one of the reasons for the development of swimming pools for racehorses. They can be worked in the pool without causing damage to the legs. It is the effect that torsion and concussion have upon the joint-binding structures that is so damaging to immature individuals.

However, stockmen and horsemen of yesterday were well aware that two- and three-year-olds were not suitable for hard work. They sometimes broke their colts to ride at two and three, but then turned them out to pasture until five. Practical experience rather than modern science and veterinary medicine dictated that they allow their horses to reach maturity before asking them to do the kinds of jobs that required maturity. Actually, they felt a five-year-old was young enough, considered six or seven closer to prime, with eight to ten years of age a physical peak.

Although modern medicine proves how right the practices of yesterday's horsemen were, modern practices of horse promotion seem to ignore the fact that lasting damage is done to horses working too hard while too young.

Many leg unsoundnesses are the result of strain and concussion on young, immature tissues. As the body matures, the connecting and supporting tissues develop strength. Modern research has shown the horse does not reach 100 percent of his body development until 5 years or 60 months of age. The kinds of injuries most frequently occurring as a result of strain to tendons, ligaments, and periosteum (bone covering) are bucked shins, bowed tendons, splints, epiphysitis, chipped knees, sesamoid fracture, ringbone, curb, bog and bone spavin, and thoroughpin.

Concussion also causes carpel and fetlock filling, navicular bursitis, stone bruises, road founder, and sidebones.

The list is by no means complete; however, without exception, the occurence of these unsoundnesses could be lessened if horses were adequately aged before being worked.

Knowing that the trend of overusing young horses is increasing in other events—and aware of the consequences—experienced competitive and endurance ride managements throughout the United States have made an effort to protect horses in distance riding by not allowing them to compete until they are at least five years old. (Some competitive rides allow four-year-olds on shortened courses involving less stress.)

Horses started even later in life, around eight to ten, are not only able to continue in competition considerably longer, but also evidence much more endurance than five- and six-year-olds.

It takes a lot of work to train and season top competitive and endurance horses. When properly managed, they can be campaigned successfully for a long time. Since lameness can be responsible for the retirement of many distance horses, it makes good sense to avoid unnecessary causes including the major problem of starting them on the distance trail prematurely.

SECTION III

COMBINED TRAINING AND EVENTING

How to Get Started in Combined Training

By
PATTY MONTALI

Reprinted from *Horse Play* Magazine by permission of the Maryland Horse Breeders Association. Subscriptions: 50B Ridge Road, Greenbelt, Maryland 20770. $12 per year.

On the big day, Mrs. Beginner approached the event secretary with a cheery smile and indicated her daughter trotting around on her horse. "We thought we'd try eventing," she explained, "what do we do?"

What Mrs. Beginner and her daughter didn't realize was that this question should have been asked *months* ago. This would have allowed time to find out what combined training is all about and to train to some level of proficiency before entering.

There are many people who would like to participate, but like Mrs. Beginner, aren't really sure what is involved or how to go about the whole thing. In fact, many people who *do* compete don't know how events are scored or many of the rules.

A combined training event (also called three-phase event or horse trial) consists of three tests. In each test the competitor is given a score based on the number of penalties he acquires. At the end of the day the winner is the one with the lowest number of penalty points in all three phases.

The first test is *dressage*. This requires the performance of certain movements on the flat in a ring 66 feet by 132 feet enclosed by a fence about 16 inches high. The ring is marked with letters at which various exercises must be performed. The American Horse Shows

Association makes up the tests and they are available from that organization for a small fee. They also come with the United States Combined Training Association's Omnibus (a schedule of events for the year).

The second test is *endurance* or cross-country. Here horse and rider must negotiate a series of jumps over a measured distance within a prescribed time. Jumps are flagged and the rider must pass with the red flag on his right and the white flag on his left. This phase is probably the favorite of most competitors. It is very much like hunting. You must jump many different types of obstacles uphill and downhill with ditches and water jumps. Some are wide, some are drops, some are combinations. There is a judge at every obstacle along the way to record each horse's performance.

The third test is *stadium jumping*. The competitor must ride a course of painted show jumps within a prescribed time. In the stadium as well as cross-country phase, only the negotiation of the fence is counted. Penalties may come from refusals, or falls, or, in the stadium phase, knockdowns. Equitation does not count but obviously good form is a useful tool.

The point of a combined training event is to produce a versatile horse—one that is calm, supple and obedient for dressage, an athletic jumper with stamina and courage for cross-country, and one able to handle a course of stadium jumps with suppleness and energy after the rigors of the cross-country.

All this sounds like a pretty tall order but it is accomplished in degrees. Levels for competition start with the Novice or Pre-training. If you are not an experienced rider or if your horse is green, this is the best place to begin. A very simple short dressage test (Training Test I) is used. It calls for a working trot and canter with simple changes of direction. The cross-country and stadium fences are usually about two feet nine inches with the cross-country about a mile in length and ridden at a hunting pace.

Most combined training events are held in one day and contain the three phases listed above. The ultimate is the Three-Day Event. As the name suggests, it is spread out over three days. The first day is devoted to the dressage test. The second is the endurance test, which is quite a bit more extensive than at the one-day level. For example, the endurance test will include four phases—a steeplechase, a cross-country over fences, two "roads and tracks" segments, where ground is covered without jumps. All this is done within a time limit. Horses are checked periodically by a veterinarian to make sure they are in condition to continue. The final day is stadium jumping.

As in any sport, you must know the rules in order to participate with the fullest enjoyment. Fifteen dollars a year will make you a member of the USCTA (United States Combined Training Association). You will receive newsletters, an Omnibus schedule, and, most importantly, a rule book. This book will answer most of your questions. A supplemental book, *Notes on Dressage and Combined Training*, discusses the dressage tests in more detail and gives other information on competing. It costs $2.50 and can be obtained from the American Horse Shows Association. Both books should be kept on hand for reference.

You would be wise to place yourself under a teacher experienced in combined training. This will get you off on the right track. Together you can set up a training schedule. Generally a horse should be worked six days a week and given one day off. His training should include dressage, jumping, and conditioning, but not all on the same day. Don't repeatedly ride the dressage test or your horse will anticipate the movements. Also, the border around a dressage ring is low, so it is advisable to practice in one before any competition. Horses new to the short sides tend to ignore them and may step out, causing you to be eliminated.

You will have to spend time conditioning your horse so he is fit enough to compete at the level you choose. If your horse comes off the cross-country blowing and sweating excessively or takes a long time to cool out, he is not fit.

Slow work at all three gaits up and down hills is very good for building muscles. Hunting, too, is excellent preparation. On the trail, take advantage of natural obstacles such as water and ditches.

Preparing for stadium jumping will probably require some cavalletti work, and practice over courses. Be sure to practice what your horse does *not* do well. Too many riders tend to do all the things the horse does best because it is more fun than working on his faults.

Now, look at your Omnibus, which lists events offered and tells you where to write for prize lists and entry blanks. The Omnibus includes entry blanks, dressage tests and information on entry fees, time schedules, divisions, accommodations, and directions to each event. Plan ahead. Don't wait until the last minute to enter, as events at the lower levels can take only a limited number of riders. They fill fast.

When you've decided where you want to compete, be sure to read and abide by the conditions set down by the organizers. Several days before the event you must call the secretary to find out the time scheduled for you to ride your dressage and cross-country tests This also confirms that you are going to the event.

The day before the event is very important. Make a list and prepare all the equipment you will need to take including buckets, sweat scrapers, coolers, extra girth and reins, and other things you might not have had to take to horse shows. Your tack, clothes, and boots should be spotless. Most horses are not given heavy work the day before an event so they'll be fresh the next day.

On the day of the event, when you arrive at the grounds, go to the secretary and pick up your number, a time schedule, and map of the cross-country course (if you have not already done so). It's a good idea to walk the course the day before. Arrive in plenty of time to let your horse have a look around and warm-up sufficiently for the dressage test. You must be on time for your tests or you may be eliminated. As the rider before you leaves the dressage ring, you may ride around the outside of the ring past the judges stand located at *C*. Many green horses find this a particularly terrifying image, so use this time to show it to your horse. Then the judge will blow a whistle or ring a bell after which you have 60 seconds to come into the ring and halt at *X*. This is usually more time than it seems, so don't panic. Make a straight relaxed entrance at *A*. It is better to have memorized your test but it is possible to have someone read it to you while you're performing.

Hunting attire is the dress for dressage and stadium jumping. A black coat, white stock tie, black velvet hard hat, white or canary breeches, and black boots are a good initial investment. Loud-colored coats and Newmarket boots are not proper. Being pressed and polished makes a good impression. In the dressage phase, a simple snaffle bit must be used, with or without a dropped noseband. Double bridles may *not* be used in dressage until the advanced level. Neither are whips, martingales, boots, nor bandages allowed.

Be sure you know each fence on the cross-country course so you can anticipate problems and be ready to cope with them. Wear a big-faced watch with a second hand. Know how much time you have to complete the course. You gain nothing by finishing many minutes early. Pace your horse and try to finish just under the minimum time. Chaps and blue jeans may not be worn but you may take off your coat and wear a jersey if you like. A hard hat is mandatory. Standing martingales are about the only piece of equipment outlawed in the jumping phases. Common eliminations occur when you don't pass through flags properly, omit jumps, or start before the signal is given. Also, unlike the dressage phase, someone on the ground helping in some way during the cross-country will cause elimination. The exception occurs when a rider has fallen and may need help catching his horse, adjusting his saddlery, and remounting. The rider must then return to the exact spot the fall occurred before resuming the course.

These are only some of the rules and suggestions for the novice interested in combined training. The fun of it is that neither horse nor rider need be conformation Thoroughbreds. Many breeds are represented, as performance is the requirement.

Go watch an event. Undoubtedly you will be inspired to get on old Blue and give it a try.

The Exciting Sport of Eventing

By
JEREMY BEALE

PART I: TRAINING FOR THE EVENT

If you have an ambition to compete over fences, but your horse is not the show ring type, combined training may be the sport for you. If hunter shows are tame and boring, combined training will provide the thrills you seek.

It costs a little more to enter a combined training event than to enter a single class at a horse show, but you get more for your money. In a horse show class you jump eight fences and you're finished. In a combined training event, you perform a dressage test, ride a cross-country course of more than a mile with about 15 obstacles, and jump a stadium course in the ring.

Combined training originated as a military competition for officers' chargers. Dressage tested their ability to perform obediently and with precision on the parade ground; cross-country tested ability to travel with speed over long distances, dealing boldly with obstacles on the way. The final phase, stadium jumping, demonstrated whether the horse was still fit and supple enough to carry on.

Now the United States Combined Training Association and many local and state organizations sponsor dozens of combined training events every year. Five levels of proficiency allow everyone from first-timer to Olympic rider to compete. An objective scoring system makes it possible for any horse to win, regardless of breed or conformation.

The levels of combined training competition begin with Novice and progress through Train-

English-born Jeremy Beale has competed at all major European events, winning enough to finance his riding on prize money alone. (Photo by Alix Coleman.)

ing, Preliminary, Intermediate, and finally Advanced, the standard for international and Olympic events.

A single event may offer competitions at three consecutive levels. Usually the three phases of a Novice or Training event are conducted all in one day, while events at the three highest levels may be spread over three days, with a separate day for each phase. In a Three-Day Event, the cross-country test is sometimes as long as 20 miles including two separate jumping courses.

The Horse You'll Need

If you aspire to compete at the advanced level you'll need a very special kind of horse. A Thoroughbred is best suited for speed and stamina and you must have a bold talented jumper to deal with big, unyielding fences even when tired. He should have substance, temperament and a beautiful way of moving to give him an edge in the dressage phase. That's a tall order.

But, at the Novice level, almost any horse that's born can compete and win. You'll see all kinds of horses: big ones, little ones, ponies, Arabians, Thoroughbreds, Appaloosas. Any horse has as good a chance as the next one.

What You'll Have To Do

All that will be expected of you at the Novice level is to perform an elementary dressage test, one of the AHSA Training Level Tests. (The terminology is confusing. When you reach Training Level you will perform a First Level dressage test.) The Training test for a Novice event consists of walk, trot, and canter both directions of a rectangular arena measuring 20 meters by 40 meters, (66′ x 132′), plus large circles using the full width and half the length of the arena (20 meter circles), and changes of direction across the diagonal. At the end of your ride you will receive a score sheet showing your score for each segment of the test, your total score and helpful comments from the judge.

The only riding sport that gives you three chances to compete for one entry fee.

The dressage test must be ridden in a plain snaffle bit with a jointed or straight-bar mouthpiece. If you use a twisted or wire bit you will be disqualified. Your horse may not wear boots or a martingale in the dressage phase of the event and only one noseband. A dropped noseband is permitted but a figure-eight, considered two nosebands in one, is barred. If you carry a whip or riding crop or if your horse steps outside the low boundary markers of the arena during the test you will be disqualified.

The cross-country course in a Novice event will probably be a little more than a mile long with about 15 obstacles. The terrain will be rolling and varied. You may go through woods, as well as fields, cross a stream or a shallow pond. The jumps themselves, which in a Novice level event may not exceed 2′9″, are modeled after obstacles which might be found in nature, but course designers are always trying to dream up interesting novelties. You won't find painted rails or barrels on the cross-country course, but you might jump a small barnyard wagon. Fences are often constructed in combination with natural features of the land: at the top of a bank, in the middle of a stream, on the far side of a ditch. Especially at the higher levels, course designers like to offer options. The rider will have to decide whether to alter course (losing time) to jump the obstacle at the lowest or easiest point, or save ground by jumping at a more difficult spot. It means that a less brave rider may take on the same fence as a bolder rider on a more experienced horse. The rider who thinks how to present the horse properly to the fence has the advantage.

Major Beale demonstrates some of the basic dressage movements with a horse in the third week of training. It shows how much can be accomplished in a short time with an apt pupil.

But the fences on a Novice course will be set so they give you a fair approach. They shouldn't be too trappy nor the turns too tight because at this level the aim is to encourage bold jumping and confidence in both horse and rider.

In the cross-country phase you must, of course, complete the flagged course which means you must get to the other side of every obstacle. Your horse's jumping style, whether he rubs the fence, or even knocks it down, doesn't matter. (The fences are solid so knock-downs are infrequent.) You'll be penalized only for fall of horse or rider, refusals, for going off course or for not completing the course in the time allowed. Some Novice events

Eventing is the only riding sport that gives you three chances to compete for one entry fee. (Photo by Alix Coleman.)

Dressage

Cross-Country

Stadium Jumping

don't have any time limit at all, and the ones that do give you plenty of leeway. Unless you fall off and have to chase your horse back to the vans to catch him, you can easily complete the course at a brisk canter. At the higher levels the time allowed gets tighter and bonus points awarded for speed become an important factor in the scoring.

The final phase, stadium jumping, is over a course of fences in the ring. The fences are jumper-type unlike the natural obstacles of the cross-country, but not designed as a high-jumping test. The stadium fences are the same height as the cross-country, 2′9″ for Novice, and the course is longer and more winding than you would normally find in a jumper competition. The purpose of the stadium phase is to show that the horse can still function athletically after his big effort on the cross-country course.

Stadium jumping scores the same errors as cross-country, with one addition. Knockdowns are penalized, too.

The relative importance of the three phases varies, but in all levels cross-country is most heavily weighted in the scoring, followed by dressage and then stadium jumping.

Preparing for the Event

If your horse is being ridden more or less every day, is capable of jumping three feet and has done some jumping out across country, you can have him ready for a Novice event in six weeks.

If he's really soft, been out to pasture or laid up, it will take you more than six weeks to get him fit because you'll have to start more slowly.

If all his jumping has been in a ring, you'll need more than six weeks to build up his confidence jumping cross-country. You can teach a horse the elements of stadium jumping in six weeks if he's never jumped a competition-type fence, but I've had a lot of experience with the show hunter type that's never been asked to jump cross country and they just don't know how to handle themselves until they're taught.

The horse is moving very nicely in the canter for this stage of training although he is not yet completely on the bit. (Photo by Alix Coleman.)

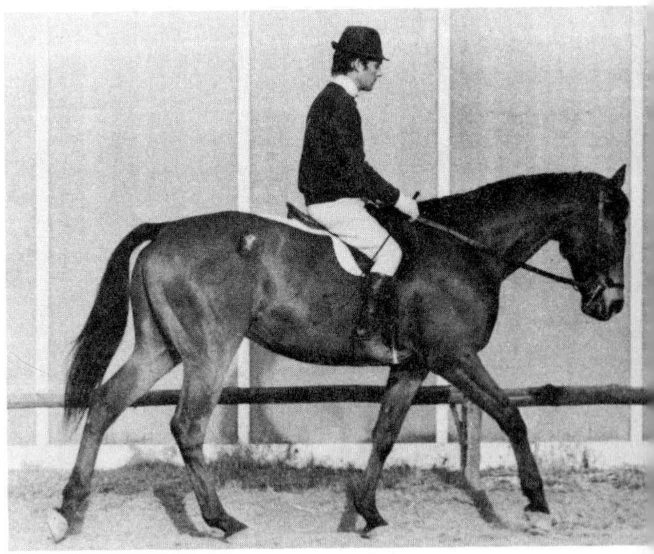

Horse and rider caught in an unhappy moment in the trot. The horse's head is too high and he is resisting the rider. (Photo by Alix Coleman.)

Major Beale demonstrates some of the basic dressage movements with a horse in the third week of training. It shows how much can be accomplished in a short time with an apt pupil.

Now the horse is beginning to accept the bit correctly in the trot while completely unrestricted in the head and neck. He is showing a rounder form and his hind leg steps much further under than in the photo above. It would be difficult to find a novice horse moving in a better frame. (Photo by Alix Coleman.)

Put in your entry just as soon as you decide to compete. Combined training events, unlike horse shows, have to limit entries because of the time it takes to judge each dressage ride. If you put it off you may be disappointed.

If this is the first time in a combined training event for you and your horse, you may have a choice of divisions. Some events offer a division for Novice Horses, some for Novice Riders; some offer a single division for Novice Horses and Novice Riders but many offer a separate division for each. If you have a choice to make, Novice Rider is probably the softest spot. In Novice Horse you may run up against top riders starting their inexperienced but very talented young horses.

At most events a horse is eligible for Novice Horse until it has completed three events and a rider is eligible for Novice Rider until he has completed three events. Any horse can compete in Novice Rider and any rider can compete in Novice Horse.

Once horse and rider reach Training level, promotions are based on the experience of the horse. When a horse has placed fifth or better three times at his current level he moves up and the rider goes with him. But when a horse has been out of competition for a long time, or when he is acquired by a new rider, the rider may apply to the United States Combined Training Association for permission to drop back one level. If the new rider is a novice, then he automatically drops back to Novice Rider, if he wishes.

A Training Program

For the next six weeks plan on riding about an hour and a half a day, six days a week. The first half hour will be devoted to work on the flat and over fences in the ring. The last hour will be spent in conditioning.

The fascinating thing about preparing a horse for combined training competition is in trying to achieve the right balance in his work according to his type, temperament and degree of experience. The racy little Thoroughbred keeps itself pretty fit and doesn't need the same amount of conditioning as the fat half-breed that gets very stuffy in his wind. A horse that is naturally very high strung may require a great deal more work in dressage than a horse that is naturally amenable.

Dressage. Four days a week, the first half hour should be spent preparing for the dressage test. Find a place to work in a ring or a field where the ground is level, and where you can mark off a rectangle the size of a dressage arena.

When your horse comes out of his stall the first thing you have to do is limber him up just as an athlete would limber up before making any great demands on his physique. Walk for three or four minutes on a long rein. Then, for the next three or four minutes, still on a long rein, work in a nice, free rising trot in both directions using the full arena.

Now, shorten the reins so you pick up a little more contact with the horse's mouth and push him forward a little more from behind. You don't want him to go any faster but to work more energetically with his hind legs, bringing them more underneath himself so as to improve his balance. What we want to see is the horse moving freely forward with a light gay step, maintaining an even rhythm and bending in the direction of the movement. He is expected to accept a steady contact but he is not required to go on the bit at the Novice level. What we don't want is a sleepy kind of an attitude with the head stuck out a mile in front and the hind legs back in the next county.

A good exercise for encouraging the horse to move his hind legs further underneath himself is to trot him on a 20 meter circle, (66 feet). Work in both directions and try to keep the horse's body bent in the direction of the circle.

You should post to the trot until the horse is warmed up. If you sit down on him while he's still stiff, he'll only stiffen more, the opposite of what you are trying to achieve. But now you can begin to work in sitting trot which gives you the advantage of being able to use your legs all the time to encourage the hind legs to move with greater energy.

When the horse is bending nicely and moving in a good even rhythm, go to work on transitions from walk to trot and trot to walk. On a long side of your arena, try a transition from working trot to strong trot by encouraging the horse to lengthen his trotting stride without

These two photographs were taken at almost the identical moment in the trotting stride. Both show the horse turning on a large circle. Above, the horse is bending correctly and obviously much better balanced than in the photograph below, where he's bent to the outside.

increasing the tempo or hurrying. You won't be asked to perform strong trot at the Novice level, but the downward transition from strong trot to working trot is a very good exercise because it makes the horse come under with his hind legs and balance himself.

Your transitions should be prompt with no sign of resistance from the horse, but smooth, never abrupt. In the downward transition from trot to walk, the horse shouldn't collapse almost to a standstill so that you have to get him going again in the walk. As you slow him with your hands, use your legs to keep him going so that he steps right out of the trot into the walk without losing forward movement. The same is true of upward transitions. When you go from trot to canter, the horse should step right into the canter without scrambling in the trot for a few steps first.

You probably shouldn't canter for the first two or three days until you feel your horse has established his balance in the trot and is capable of making downward transitions without offering too much resistance to your hand. The canter is a very difficult pace for the horse to balance in. It is so different from the trot and so similar to the gallop that the horse tends to get a little strong and excitable.

Avoid cantering down the long side at first where he may get strong. Rather, start your cantering on the 20 meter circle. Don't ask him to sustain the canter for very long initially. If he starts to become unbalanced it may lead to disagreement between horse and rider. As soon as you feel him get a little strong bring him back to the trot.

When the horse is nicely balanced in the canter you can begin to work on transitions from trot to canter and canter to trot. At this stage don't attempt more than one transition at a time. Don't try to go from walk to canter or canter to walk without trotting for a little while in between.

Above all, keep the work interesting for the horse by varying it. Make a circle, cross the diagonal and make another circle at the other end, then, try some transitions down the long side.

It is unwise to practice the dressage test itself more than once or twice before the event because your horse will start to anticipate. But you should practice all the movements out of sequence. There is no point in losing points needlessly because your circle is the wrong size or not round, or you don't know where to change the rein.

It may seem that we're taking too much trouble over dressage when it forms a relatively small part of the scoring, but the benefits from preparation on the flat will be felt throughout the horse's performance.

Jumping. We said that on four of your six riding days of the week, you'll spend the first half hour working on dressage. On the other two days, after a few minutes of warming up on the flat, the first half hour should be devoted to jumping.

We're not teaching your horse to jump. We assume he is already jumping three feet, but now we want to accustom him to some of the strange fences he'll encounter in the stadium jumping phase. He must learn to use himself properly over his fences, to adjust his stride going through combinations and keep his balance around turns. The benefits will carry over to his jumping on the cross-country course.

Start with three or four fences placed at random around the ring. Build them from whatever unusual materials you can find: spools, barrels, tires, even a piece of polyethylene laid underneath to simulate water. Paint the rails with bright stripes. You should have some upright fences but mostly spreads and square fences (spreads with front and back elements at the same height). Square fences are very good preparation for any kind of jump because they really teach a horse to use himself.

Start the fences very low so that the horse becomes accustomed to them and confident. Jump them at random, varying the order, sometimes circling in between so that the horse

To prepare for the cross-country, take advantage of any little obstacle you come upon. The horse is jumping the fallen tree a little too extravagantly but this is typical of a novice horse. Ditches and water should be jumped high, wide and bold, and the horse above is doing just that.

practices turning and approaching from different directions.

Introduce your horse to combinations, double and triple in-and-outs, starting with cavaletti or very low fences. If the fences are low enough he shouldn't have much problem. As he progresses, build up a course and make your fences higher until he is jumping the full height required at the event.

Conditioning. The remaining hour each day is devoted to riding out in the country to prepare for the cross-country phase. The course will be little more than a mile. Your horse doesn't have to be dead fit, but, to perform well, he should be in good working condition, his wind developed and his muscles hard.

First Two Weeks: Four days in the week, go out for a trail ride. Combine walking and trotting so that you average about six miles an hour. While you're out in the country look for odd little obstacles, logs, ditches, but nothing big. The object is to develop confidence in the horse and teach him to handle himself in tricky situations. I'm not a believer in jumping big cross-country fences, in cold blood, shortly before a competition. There's too much risk involved. Your horse knows how to jump; that should be behind you. All you want to do now is give him self-confidence in dealing with the unexpected and put some variety in his work to help him enjoy it.

On the other two working days, give your horse a hand gallop of about a mile. Find a field where the footing is good, no holes, rocks, bogs or steep grades, and measure out a mile course. Avoid sharp corners and look for long straightaways so your horse isn't always turning. Don't overdo the pace. It shouldn't be much more than a brisk canter of about 10 or 12 miles an hour. On the days that you canter use the half hour of ring work as a warmup, and then skip or very much shorten the trail work. Afterwards take him for a walk to cool him out until he's finished blowing.

Third Week: The trail work is the same, but step up the two fast works. Keep the distance at a mile but send him at a strongish gallop, about 18 miles an hour. If he's the habitually lazy type, try to find a friend to gallop beside you so that your horse gets a little bit competitive. Don't ever push him so fast that he can't go any faster. He should always stay in your hand.

Fourth Week: Same routine except, for the second fast work, gallop the mile course twice with a 20 to 30 minute walk in between. The second time around your horse should feel stronger and really raring to go.

Fifth Week: Repeat the routine of the fourth week, but this time both your fast works should be two one-mile gallops with a 20 or 30 minute walk in between.

Final Week: Cut your trail rides to three-quarters of an hour or even less, so that you can concentrate on your schooling in the ring. Keep him tuned up with two short sharp gallops, each a very fast seven furlongs (⅞ of a mile). The second gallop should be on the day before the event.

PART II: WALKING THE COURSE

Since this is presumably your first try at combined training, try to find an event close enough to your home so that you won't have to worry about overnight stabling. If you go away for the night you must take a lot of extra equipment plus feed, possibly hay, and even water if your horse is fussy about drinking in strange places. You'll feel better if you can make all your preparations, do your grooming and braiding, at home, and your horse will be in a better frame of mind and sleep better the night before if he spends it at home in his stall.

On the day before the event, get your riding out of the way in the morning and plan to devote the afternoon to walking the cross-country course. Not only will you be terribly rushed if you have to walk the course on the day of the event, but this preliminary trip gives you an opportunity to familiarize yourself with the layout, learn which of the several dressage arenas you'll be riding in, and find out your starting time so you'll know exactly what time to arrive the next morning. Not the least important benefit is that you find out how to get there and how long it will take.

What to Expect of the Course

The cross-country course in a Novice level event will probably cover a little more than a mile of ground and consist of about 15 obstacles. Many of the obstacles will incorporate natural features like banks, ditches, streams and woods. The first fence will probably be something inviting, like a brush obstacle, to get you going. After that, expect each fence to pose some kind of problem that should be worked out beforehand. In a Novice level course, the problems will be relatively simple and none of the fences should be exceptionally tricky or forbidding because the object at the lower levels is to develop confidence in both horse and rider. But nevertheless you should devote some thought to the best way to negotiate every obstacle.

The course will be marked and all the ob-

Three fences which, although above Novice level difficulty, demonstrate ways in which course designers capitalize on shifting terrain. (Photos by Alix Coleman.)

Steps are one way of getting up a steep slope.

A fence with a drop on the landing side.

Two fences complicated by a steep downhill slope.

Two good reasons for walking every step of the course. The simple fence above has a small stream underneath which couldn't be seen from a distance. The horse is clearly alarmed, and if the rider hadn't been prepared, she might have had a refusal.

This is a fence which presents a choice of four panels. You have to stand up to this fence to know which part is most jumpable. It would be easy to have a run-out here if you didn't have your choice firmly in mind. (Photos by Alix Coleman.)

stacles will be indicated with red and white flags. A pair of flags will mark the start, another pair, the finish, and when the course departs from a straight line between obstacles, in order to add extra distance, there will be turning flags you must go around. The rule to remember is: red flags on the right, white flags on the left. If you err from the flagged course you are eliminated unless you rectify the error.

Providing you stay on course, what you do between obstacles, bearing in mind that the clock keeps ticking, is your own business. But what you do within range of the flagged obstacles is the business of the judge stationed at each one. Every obstacle is bounded by a penalty zone which extends 10 meters (33 feet) on the take-off side, 20 meters (66 feet) on landing and 10 meters (33 feet) to left and right. The penalty zone is usually marked with small white pegs, paint or chalk. Within the penalty zone any slip-up counts against you.

You'll lose points for fall of horse and/or rider, for stepping backward, for recrossing your own line and for leaving the penalty zone without attempting to jump the obstacle. Refusals and runouts are penalized, of course, because they involve either stepping backward or crossing your own line to take another shot at the fence, but you will not be penalized twice if you leave the penalty zone in order to represent your horse after a refusal. Three errors, refusals, runouts, or falls, at any one obstacle, eliminates. But unlike most competition over fences, in which a total of three errors eliminates, you can accumulate up to two refusals on every obstacle and still complete the course.

What to Do When You Get There

The cross-country fences will all be flagged and numbered consecutively, and you'll probably be given a map showing their location. Walk the course twice, first quickly for a preliminary appraisal and then more slowly the second time, to make a final plan. You have to know where you're going and what is still to come to judge where on the course you should save your horse and where you should send him on to make time.

Begin at the starting flags and walk every step of the course. Don't take shortcuts. There could be a hidden hazard, a stream or a ditch at the foot of an obstacle, that can't be seen from a distance. But whether there is a hazard or not, you can't judge the best way to negotiate an obstacle without studying the obstacle and surrounding terrain close up.

Take a careful look at the approach. If it's downhill, remember that you will have to take special pains to steady your horse or he may sprawl down the hill and meet the fence off balance. If the approach is uphill, you may have to ride a little more strongly than usual to be sure your horse arrives at the fence with enough impulsion to get over. Take a careful look at the ground right in front of the fence. It may be a little higher or smoother in one spot, offering a better take-off. The fence itself, because of the natural contours of the ground, may be a little lower on one side than the other.

What about the landing side? Will you gallop on or will you have to make a sudden turn to negotiate another obstacle or to avoid a tree? If you are faced with the prospect of an abrupt change of direction immediately after the obstacle, you may decide to trot into it so that your momentum doesn't carry you off course.

All these decisions should be made with your horse in mind. If he's a bold galloping horse, take advantage of his ability to cover ground in the open, but in the trappy places, choose a spot for him to negotiate the obstacle that gives him the widest possible turning radius and plan to trot, or at least, use a controlled canter.

If your horse is the careful, clever kind, he'll be right at home in the tricky spots and his handiness around turns may take seconds off your time. (I wouldn't encourage anybody at the Novice level to plan to jump at an angle in order to save ground.) But he may need an extra strong ride into the spread fences, especially if they're the type that might put him off. A trakener, for example, a fence over a ditch,

Three typical Novice level fences, no tricks, and nothing exceeding 2′9″. (Photos by Alix Coleman.)

You're bound to encounter water somewhere on the course. Course designers handle it in a variety of ways. You may jump in, upper left; or over, upper right; or in and then out, left; or you may encounter an obstacle like the log at the right with both take-off and landing in water. (Photos by Alix Coleman.)

demands momentum but a careful horse may want a close look at the ditch.

Every obstacle offers the rider options. He decides exactly where he wants to meet it, from what angle and at what pace. But some obstacles are designed with just that object in mind, to offer the rider two or more very distinct choices. It is up to the rider to choose the course best suited to his horse. Usually the choice is between a direct route which requires the boldest jumping effort but saves on time, and an easier jumping problem but a longer route. For example, you might come down a hill to find a stream with a fence on the other side. The fence is set at an angle, close to the stream on the left but sloping 20 or 30 feet away on the right. If you have a bold horse, you can gallop down the hill (taking care to steady your horse so that he doesn't sprawl), and meet the left side of the obstacle, clearing stream and fence with one leap. That would be the shortest, swiftest route and require the biggest jumping effort. The alternative, with a less bold but handy horse, is to aim for the right side of the obstacle. Let your horse pick his way through the stream, trot a few strides on the opposite bank and pop over the fence. It's a slower, but for some, safer course. As a general guide, however, my advice is that boldest is best. When you take the circuitous route, not only do you lose time, but your horse may be set for the portion of the obstacle directly ahead. When you turn him away to an easier spot, he's caught by surprise, his balance and his concentration are disturbed and you may have a refusal.

When you walk the course be alert for the special problems posed by two or more fences near each other. Sometimes two or three neighboring fences are considered a combination, technically one obstacle, and if so, they will be numbered accordingly. Three fences, if they form a combination, will be a, b and c of the same number, for example, 12a, 12b, and 12c. If they're separate fences, they'll be numbered 12, 13 and 14. Make sure you note which are the combinations because different

These are course designers' favorites, although neither is truly a natural obstacle. Above, a picnic table; below, an adaptation of the famous "Cat's Cradle" on the Badminton course in England. It consists of two triangles, meeting at their tips, and offers the rider a number of alternatives. The most direct route is to jump in at the base, jump the X-shaped fence where the tips meet, which this rider is doing, and jump out the other base. It's also possible to move right or left, jumping a corner of each triangle, which would involve only two fences, each a spread. If you look closely you'll see each triangle has an open gate. Other alternatives involve the gates and simpler jumping problems but time-consuming changes of direction. (Photos by Alix Coleman.)

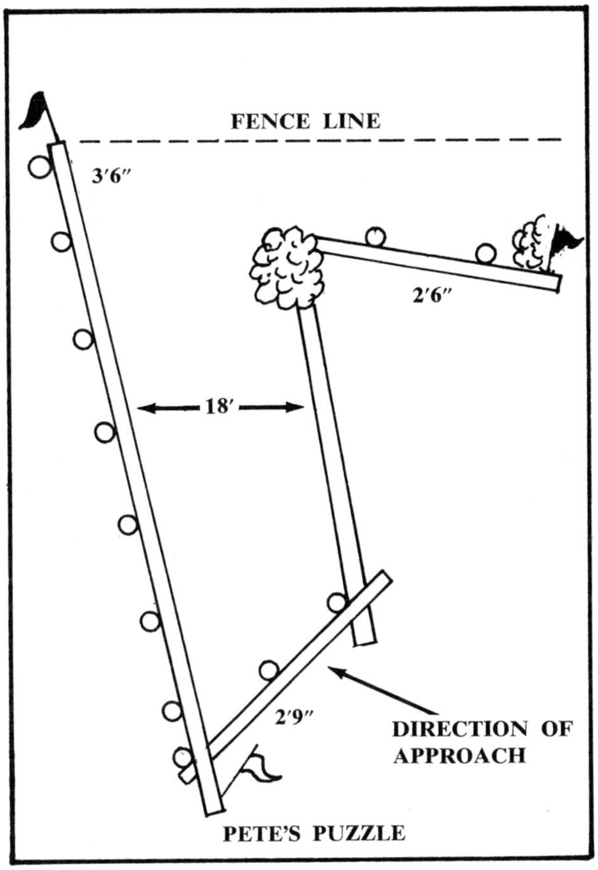

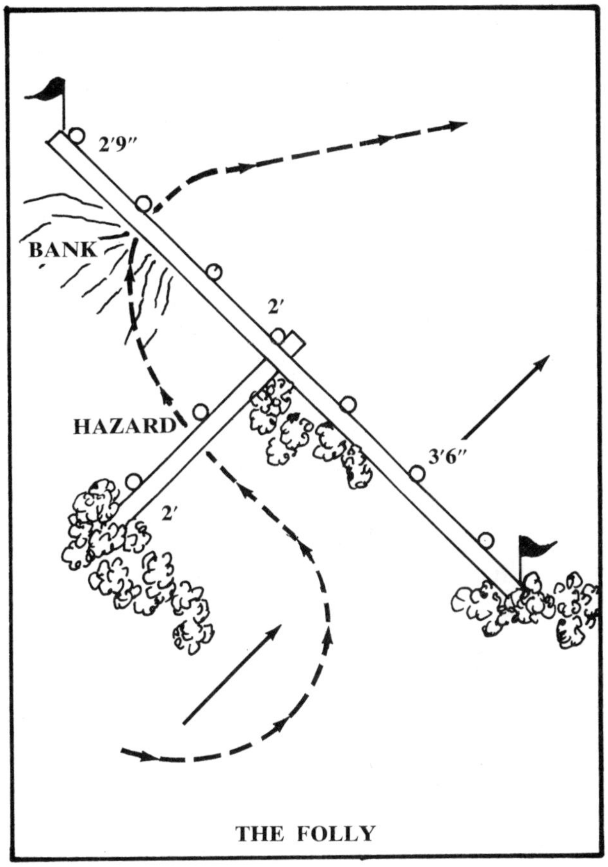

Plans for two fences designed by Major Beale, both offering the rider interesting alternatives. Left, there are three ways of tackling "Pete's Puzzle." The direct approach is the corner by the white flag, taken in one jump. The rather tight 18′ in-and-out is one possibility; another is to jump in over the 2′6″ portion of the first fence, then, depending on your horse's ability, jump out over the 3′6″ panel or, losing more ground, swing left to the lower end. "The Folly," right, allows a bold rider to take a direct route over the rather large looking 3′6″ fence at the top of a bank. The alternative is to swing left, jump an unflagged 2′ fence partly hidden in bushes, and jump the flagged obstacle at a lower point. The danger here is in the risk you run of a refusal when you turn away from the fence the horse expects to jump.

rules apply. If you have a refusal at the second or third fence of a combination, you may go back and start again from the first fence, if you feel it will give your horse a better approach. But if the fences are considered separate, you must jump only the fence that caused the refusal. Retaking a fence already jumped incurs elimination.

Often, consecutive fences are so close that their penalty zones overlap. For example, two fences might actually meet in an L-shape but be considered separate obstacles. When you land over the first fence you are in the penalty zone of the second fence. Remember you will be penalized if you leave a penalty zone without completing the obstacle. You must plan your approach to the first fence very carefully so that your momentum doesn't carry you out of the penalty zone before you have a chance to get turned and jump the second fence. Your pace should be slow and, if the second fence is to your left, aim for the right side of the first fence to give yourself plenty of room to turn.

If the stream with the fence angling away to the right, that we mentioned before, was flagged as two separate obstacles, you would have a similar problem if you chose to meet them over toward the right. You would have to plan to cross the stream at an angle which would allow you to turn and make your approach to the fence without leaving the overlapping penalty zones.

As you walk the course you will probably find one or two obstacles that strike you as a little alarming. I advise you to go back and look at them a second and even a third time. You'll find that when they're familiar they don't look nearly so forbidding. Still it's perfectly natural to spend the night before an event worrying about a particular fence, and it may work to your advantage because it probably means you'll ride that fence very aggressively. But don't get so hung up on one fence that you disregard the others. You must not relax for a moment, even at a simple looking fence, because as soon as you do, you're in trouble. The simplest fences cause the most problems just because riders don't treat them with enough respect.

By the time you arrive at the finish on foot, you'll probably be puffing hard and worrying that the course is hard and long. But don't be discouraged because it will seem much less difficult to your horse than it does to you.

(Photo by Alix Coleman.)

PART III: ON THE DAY OF THE EVENT

On the day before, you made an exploratory trip to the site of the event. You walked the cross-country course and you learned your starting times for the dressage and cross-country phases. Now you know how long it will take to get there and what time you have to arrive.

If time permits, do your braiding in the morning rather than the night before. The braids will look better if they haven't been slept on and your horse will sleep more comfortably. Some high strung horses, as soon as they're braided, know something is up and worry all night. Braiding is not mandatory, but a braided mane will certainly make a better impression on the dressage judge. It is not necessary to braid the tail.

The excellent turn-out of horse and rider cannot help but make a favorable impression on the dressage judge. (Photo by Alix Coleman.)

As for your own turnout, if you have a

For the cross-country phase, the rider has taken off her coat and changed to pelham bit with martingale, all perfectly permissible. (Photo by Alix Coleman.)

black formal hunting coat, wear it. If not, at the Novice level, a tweed or muted color is perfectly acceptable. Your coat is for the dressage and stadium jumping phases. It's traditional to ride the cross-country in a turtleneck shirt as well as a hard hat with chin harness. A coat would get very hot and cumbersome.

You may wear spurs but they must be blunt and may not have rowels. You are not permitted to carry a whip in the dressage test but for cross-country and stadium you are permitted a whip no longer than 30″. I strongly recommend that you use a whip with a button top wide enough that if you have a fall, the end can't poke you in the eye.

In the dressage test your horse must wear a smooth snaffle bit. He may have a dropped noseband, but only one noseband. He is not permitted a martingale or boots. In the other two phases, you may use any bit you choose; you may use a martingale but, if FEI rules are enforced, only a running martingale. Boots are permitted. However, it has been my experience that it is preferable to wear neither boots nor bandages on the cross-country course. Boots can chafe the horse's legs especially if mud or gravel gets into them or they get wet. Bandages

These are the correct salutes for lady and gentleman, but the horse on the left may have lost points for not maintaining his halt. (Photos by Alix Coleman.)

In the warm-up before your dressage test, be sure to give your horse a good look at the judge's trailer so it doesn't alarm him during the test. (Photo by Alix Coleman.)

In the cross-country phase, if you come loose over a fence, try to hang on until you're out of the penalty zone. (Photo by Alix Coleman.)

become very soggy and heavy. They may slip down and come undone. If you must use bandages, they should be sewn in. I make one exception. If your horse tends to overreach, he should wear rubber bell boots. But even these have a habit of turning upside down in mud and may become useless.

If the morning of the event dawns wet or threatening, it is worth a phone call to the organizer to find whether the competition is postponed.

Plan to arrive at the event in enough time to warm your horse up and settle him down. You can warm him up in 10 minutes, but you may need an hour and a half to settle him down. When you arrive, go to the secretary's office to pick up your number cloth.

Do your warming up in the vicinity of the dressage arena so that your horse won't be unsettled by a change of surroundings at the last minute. But stay at least 20 meters away from the arena so that you don't disturb the competitors ahead of you.

About 10 minutes before your assigned time, report to the ring steward to let him know you're there. Then keep your horse working quietly until your turn arrives. When the competitor before you finishes his test, you are permitted to work your horse around the outside of the arena. Be sure you take advantage of the opportunity. If there's room, ride between the arena and the markers and most certainly let him see the trailer or tent where the judges are sitting so that he's not alarmed while he's doing his test.

When the judges have finished scoring the ride before yours, they will ring a bell which means that you may enter. You have 60 seconds before you must enter. The 60-second rule applies to all three phases. If you don't appear within a minute of your time you forfeit your turn. You may be allowed to go after everyone else is finished, but your score won't count.

Don't panic when the bell rings. Continue around the arena until you reach the entrance and then begin your test. If you are carrying a

Let your horse settle into stride at the start and aim at averaging a hand gallop around the course. (Photo by Alix Coleman.)

stick, don't forget to drop it or hand it to a friend before you enter.

You should know your dressage test by heart so you can put your full attention on your horse. It is perfectly acceptable, for extra insurance, to have a friend call the test out to you as you perform it.

If you do make a mistake in the test, you will hear the bell ring. Even if you realize where you went wrong, it is courteous to go up to the judges and ask them where they would like you to resume. If you try to pick up the thread on your own, you may begin in the middle of a movement, making it difficult for the judges to score you.

If you make a mistake, keep your cool; it happens to all of us. You'll lose some marks but you won't be eliminated unless you make two more.

The presentation of your test is important. It should look tidy and your horse will go better if you ride accurately. Make your circles round and of the correct size. Make sure that you don't cut corners and that your horse is bent correctly in the direction of his movement. Ride him straight on the long sides and when you change the rein ride him straight toward the markers.

Try to make your transitions smooth and prompt. If you have difficulty, make sure that you prepare in plenty of time and make your upward transitions a little on the early side. A trifle early is better than very late. In the case of downward transitions, it's common at the Novice level to have the opposite problem. If you're cantering and you think, "I'm going to trot when I get to A," you will instinctively say trot to your horse and he will trot too soon.

If you're unfortunate enough to get the wrong lead in the canter, bring your horse back to a trot immediately and try again. You'll only lose a few marks for an error quickly corrected, but for cantering left when you're supposed to canter right, you'll get no marks at all.

When making your final turn down the center line, don't wait until you arrive at A to turn. You'll overshoot the center and never get straight. Turn a little early, and if you find you're off center, you can always let your horse drift to the center as you turn.

You will be expected to salute the judges before you start your test and at the finish, as well as before you begin your stadium jumping round. A man salutes by removing his hat in his right hand and dropping his right arm to his side. A lady drops her right arm and bows her head. Many riders starting out are inclined to hurry their salutes which gives the impression they fear their horse won't stand still. It's courteous to take your time. Make sure your horse is completely halted and transfer the reins to your left hand. Hold the salute for a moment and try not to look too grim. Judges always appreciate a smile. Then unhurriedly separate the reins and move your horse forward.

After your test, leave the arena promptly and ride away from the immediate vicinity before you dismount and chat so that you'll be out of the way of other competitors. Unless you have to ride your cross-country right away, put your horse back in the trailer and let him rest. There's nothing I hate seeing more than a horse still tacked up and dragging around behind his rider when he still has the big test to come.

Keep your eye on your watch and about 40 minutes before you're due to ride the cross-country, check that it's still on schedule. Sometimes fence repairs cause delays. Then take your horse out of the trailer and start getting ready. Mount up 10 to 15 minutes before your starting time and report to the starter. Make sure you warm your horse up thoroughly. Loosen him up at the trot and then canter him in both directions for a total of about five minutes to get him breathing right and going nice and freely.

The starter will call you to the starting box when he's ready and warn you when you have a minute to go. He'll count down for you and at 30 seconds you should go into the box, if there is one, or stand at the starting flags, and wait for the signal to go. The rules require a standing start. One word of warning: if you start before the starter says go, you will have to come back and start again while the clock is ticking.

You should aim to average a hand gallop around the course. Push on where you have long stretches between fences so that you can go more slowly where you have difficult terrain. Don't hurry at the beginning. Get your horse going comfortably and try to settle him into a nice even rhythm. You certainly don't need to go as fast as you worked in the final stages of your conditioning. The time allowed at the Novice level should let you ride around at a good strong canter without worrying about time penalties.

If you have a refusal, don't despair. You'll lose points but you're not out of contention until you're eliminated and that takes three errors at one obstacle. Make your approach again without wasting any time. The only assistance you're allowed is in catching your horse and remounting after a fall. If someone helps you shoo your horse over a fence after a refusal or gives you course directions, you're eliminated. Even if you are eliminated, at the

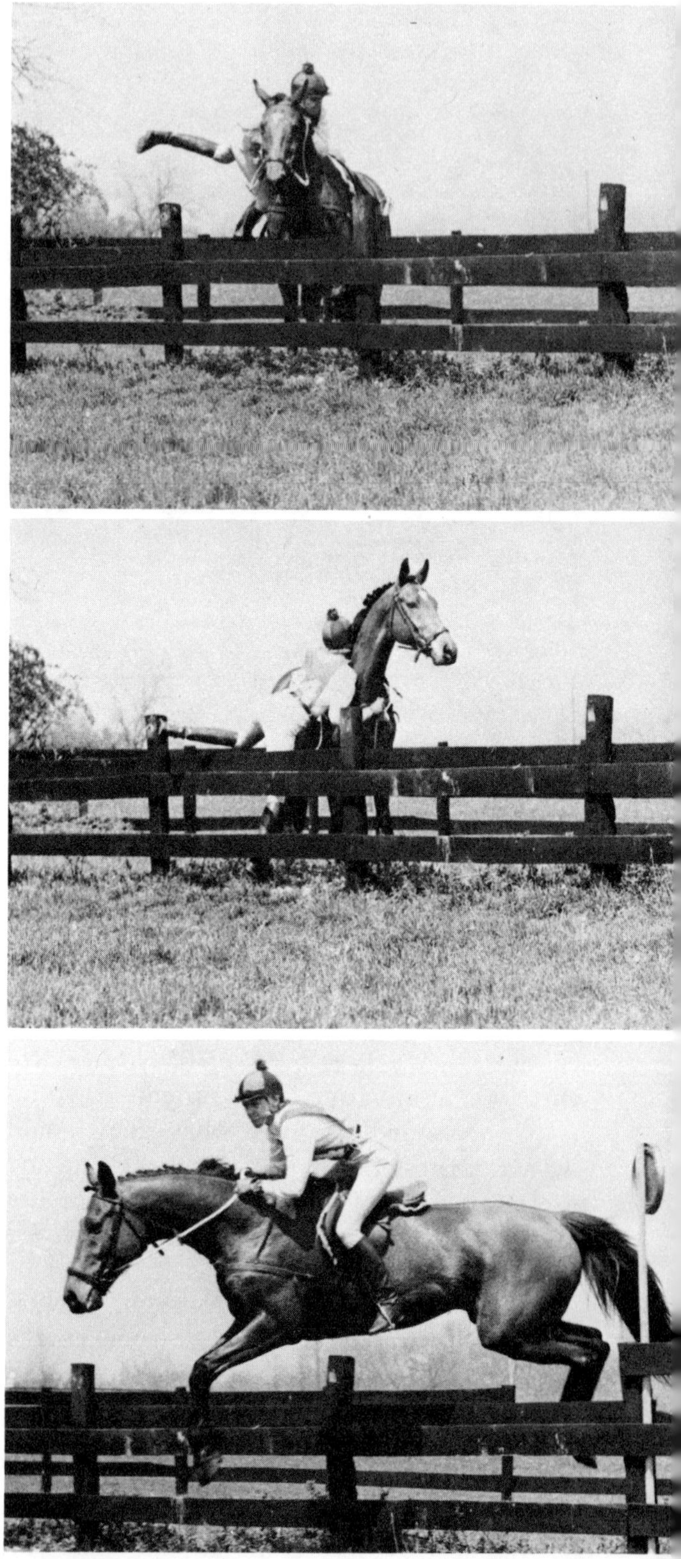

If you have a fall in the penalty zone, remount quickly and try again. With one fall or refusal you are still in the running. (Photos by Alix Coleman.)

Novice level, you will probably be permitted to complete the course if you wish.

After you've jumped the last fence, gallop on to the flags but don't make a big steeplechase finish out of it with your horse under the stick. Pull your horse up slowly over a distance of about 30 or 40 yards. If you pull him up too quickly when he's tired, you risk injuring his tendons. Jump off immediately, run your stirrups up, loosen his girth and walk him for several minutes until he stops blowing hard. Take him back to the trailer, give him a little water, but no more than half a bucket, and, weather permitting, wash him down. Walk him until he's cool and dry, give him another half bucket of water, and put him away. Come back 20 minutes later and give him as much water as he wants.

The stadium jumping course should be ready and now is the time to go inspect it. Walk every inch of the track you are going to ride so that you can see exactly where to turn in order to make a good approach to each obstacle.

Step out the distances between fences in combinations and where they come close behind one another in a straight line. You should know the length of your own stride and your horse's stride so that you can decide where you will need to ride strongly and where steady.

You must also decide whether to go strong or steady in regard to the type of fence. A triple bar or a water jump should be met with a lengthening stride. An upright fence should be ridden with a lot of impulsion but on a fairly short stride to keep your horse from flattening out or running up under. A square fence poses the problems of an upright combined with the problems of a spread. It demands the same respect as an upright fence but a slightly longer stride because of the spread.

Be sure you note the location of start and finish flags. Sometimes you'll have to turn to go through the finish. When it's not right in front of you, it's easy to forget about the finish while the clock keeps ticking.

You won't have an assigned time, but the stadium phase will begin at an appointed hour

The pace in the stadium jumping is faster than for a show jumping competition, although not as fast as required for the cross-country. Be sure to note position of start and finish flags when you walk the course. (Photos by Alix Coleman.)

and you will ride in the same order as you rode your dressage and cross-country tests. Don't be late because the one-minute rule applies.

Your pace in the stadium is not as fast as your cross-country pace but somewhat faster than for most show jumping competitions. You will have to canter on; you won't be able to keep a collected canter all the way around.

Show jumping rules apply to the stadium phase although the scoring is different. Three refusals anywhere on the whole course eliminate you. Knockdowns score heavily against you. Touches don't count. If you have a refusal at the second or third element of a combination you *must* retake the whole combination. This is different from cross-country where you *may* retake the whole combination if you choose.

After the stadium phase is finished you will have a 30 or 40 minute wait for the final scores. It will take the jump judges at the far corners of the cross-country course a while to return with their score cards, and the scoring calculations, themselves, are complicated and take time.

While you're waiting, return your number cloth to the secretary's office and pick up your dressage score sheet. If you had problems in cross-country and stadium, you know where you went wrong and you probably have a pretty good idea of how to improve next time. The judge's comments on your dressage sheet will give you some very valuable tips on how you can improve your dressage performance. By the time you find out how you scored in your first event, you will already know how to do better in your next.

Preparing to Event

By
SHEILA WALL HUNDT

Combined Training, also known as Eventing, is the horse sport which best tests the all-round skill of the horse and rider. At its simplest level, it may consist of only two tests, while at its highest level, the Three-Day Event, it consists of six tests and the overall Test in the Open may be as long as twenty miles. The origins of the sport are found in the days of the horse cavalry: the dressage was to show that the horse was calm, obedient and precise on the parade ground; the cross-country was to show that the horse and rider could travel with speed for long distances over varied terrain, jumping challenging obstacles on the way; the stadium jumping was to show that the horse was fit, sound, and supple enough to continue performing his duties. The sport, in the framework that now exists, first appeared in the Stockholm Olympics of 1912 and American teams, both military and civilian, have since seldom come home from the Olympic Games without a medal.

The Three-Day Event is the pinnacle of the sport and, because it is so strenuous a test of horse and rider, only a few are held in a year. The Horse Trial, being much less severe a test, is the base of the sport and provides the training ground for competitors of even Olympic aspirations. The *Supplement to Rules on Dressage and Combined Training*, available from the American Horse Shows Association, 527 Madison Avenue, New York, N.Y. or the United States Combined Training Association, 1 Winthrop Square, Boston, Mass., is essential to anyone interested in Eventing.

This article has been excerpted from a more extensive discussion in the book *Invitation to Riding*, 1975, published by Simon & Schuster.

It contains all the rules and standards of the various phases encompassed in Combined Training Events held in the United States that are not of international caliber. The terminology of this sport is somewhat confusing, for several different kinds of competition come under the general heading of Combined Training, but we will try to clarify some of the terms. A *Combined Training Event* may consist of two or more tests from the following: dressage, roads and tracks, cross-country, steeplechase and stadium jumping. The same horse and rider must compete in all phases that are asked for in order to be eligible for a prize.

The *dressage test* consists of a series of prescribed movements on the flat, carried out in a standard arena, in which the horse is judged on his performance according to his level of training, and the rider is judged on his position and the use of his aids. The *roads and tracks phase* requires competitors to complete a marked course (without jumps) which may range from two to ten miles at a minimum stipulated rate of speed, usually a good trot. The *steeplechase course* of one to 2½ miles in length must be covered at a strong to racing gallop over eight to twelve fences, usually made of brush. The *cross-country course* ranges from one to 4½ miles, to be covered at a rate of speed ranging from a hand gallop to a strong gallop, over varied terrain and fences such as walls, coops, timber, gates, combinations, drops, ditches, water and any combination thereof. The *stadium jumping* is carried out over a relatively short course consisting of ten to twelve show-type fences.

All phases are judged on whether the competitor completed the course in the allowed time; penalties are given for such jumping faults as refusals on the cross-country, refusals and knockdowns in the stadium jumping, and for exceeding the time allowed on any of the courses. Style is only considered in the dressage test. The competitor is eliminated for such things as three falls of horse and/or rider at obstacles on the cross-country, three refusals at the same obstacle in any phase, or for any breach of rules, such as failing to keep all red flags to the right and white flags to the left, jumping a fence out of order, failing to report to the starter at the prescribed time, etc.

The simplest combined training event is known as the *Combined Event*; it is a two-phase event usually consisting of a dressage and a stadium jumping test, but could be a combination of any two of the tests mentioned above. A *Horse Trial* is a three-phase event, usually held in one day, testing the competitor in dressage, cross-country and stadium jumping; sometimes a short roads and tracks phase is included. A full-scale *Three-Day Event*, which is also sometimes called a Horse Trial, takes place over a period of three days: the dressage test is held on the first day; the test in the open (which includes phase A, roads and tracks; phase B, steeplechase; phase C, roads and tracks; and phase D, cross-country) is held on the second day; the stadium jumping is held on the final day.

The levels of competition found in Combined Training, starting at the lowest, are Pre-training (novice), Training, Preliminary, Intermediate, Advanced (open). The Pre-training division is not recognized by the U.S. Combined Training Association, but most organizers of these events still follow the national rules closely. Guidelines for these events have been set up by the USCTA, but are not mandatory. From the training level upward, the owner of the horse must become a member of the USCTA. The member receives a rule book, periodic newsletters which contain interesting articles and photos, an Omnibus schedule of approved USCTA events for the year, and becomes eligible for year-end awards. In order to get an idea of what standards to expect for the various levels, see the chart on page 120. A combined training event is quite different from any other horse sport. It is essential that you become thoroughly familiar with the regulations in the rule book, and that you attend a couple of horse trials at the lower levels as a spectator in order to become familiar with the proceedings.

Note the attire expected in each phase: formal dress (or proper ratcatcher at the Pre-training level) for the dressage and stadium jumping tests; informal attire (chaps are not allowed) for the *cross-country*. The regulations for the dressage and stadium jumping tests are the same as those for all dressage and stadium jumping competitions. The cross-country is governed by its own body of regulations. All the information you need is contained in the *Supplement to Rules on Dressage and Combined Training*. We will not attempt to restate all the rules in this discussion as they are clearly stated in the pamphlet. If any of the rules are unclear to you, ask for an explanation from the organizer or the technical delegate of an event.

Study all phases of the competition. Watch a few dressage rides. Obtain a map and walk the cross-country course, carefully observing the types of obstacles. Spend a good deal of time watching the cross-country in progress. Note how the start and finish are conducted, then go and watch how the competitors handle some of the more difficult fences. Last, but certainly not least, observe some stadium jumping rounds. Now you can go home and school your horse in each of the three phases.

Unless you are an experienced competitor in other horse sports, you should start at the Pre-training level. Although your horse is capable of jumping the 3′3″ maximum height of the Training level fences, the courses are more difficult than this measurement may imply due to the type of obstacles and their placement. The qualifications for Pre-training are not rigid, but most state that the horse and/or rider must not have completed more than three events to be eligible. The Pre-training division may be divided into a Novice Horse and a Novice Rider section or into a Junior Pre-training and a Senior Pre-training in which either the horse or the rider must be a novice.

Having been to an event or two, you know exactly what to expect in the dressage and stadium jumping tests and have a fairly good idea of what to expect in the cross-country. The chart tells you the length, speeds and dimensions of the obstacles at the various levels, but the character of the course is dependent on what terrain and material are available to the course builder. One course may be laid out over hilly terrain providing banks and drops but possibly no water at all; another course may be on very flat terrain, not providing any drops but having several obstacles involving water or ditches. A good course provides a selection of all the basic obstacles, but this is not always possible, especially at the lower levels.

The fences should be "natural," that is of the type you would expect to find riding cross-country; walls, banks, steps, ditches, water, brush, fallen trees, gates, board and post and rails. However, the course builder may have rather innovative ideas about what is a "natural" fence: tires stacked in various patterns and aluminum drainpipes are popular. At the Pre-training and Training levels, the combinations should not be tricky, the striding should be easy, and the turns not too tight.

Accustom your horse to the basic variety of obstacles he may face before entering an event. Train him to jump strange obstacles promptly and willingly so that, when he is faced with something that is new to him, he will have the confidence to jump it willingly. School him over little ditches and banks to gain his confidence before tackling larger obstacles. If you do not have ditches or banks of the dimensions expected in the event, do not worry. A horse that will handle a four-foot ditch confidently will jump a six-foot ditch. The important thing is that a horse should recognize the type of obstacle and have the experience to handle it.

The rider can help the horse a good deal if he knows how he wants to approach the fences. The one constant to a good approach is impulsion, whether the pace be a trot or a gallop, the stride short or long. When a horse arrives at a fence with good impulsion, it is easier for him to keep going over it than it is to stop. If a horse hits a fence that he has jumped with good impulsion, he has a better chance of recovery when he lands. When determining what pace at which to tackle a difficult fence, the rider must take into consideration his horse's personality. Horses with a cautious nature need time to study an obstacle and, if hustled into a fence, may throw on the brakes at the last minute. However, most horses gain confidence from a strong, steady approach. But whatever the pace—impulsion, impulsion, impulsion!

You need not worry about getting to a precise point for takeoff on the cross-country course, particularly at the lower levels where the obstacles are low and/or relatively narrow. Make the basic decision on whether the situation calls for a short, bouncy stride or for a longer, freer stride and let the horse sort it out for himself. Short combinations, obstacles followed by a sharp turn, downhill fences, drops, banks, steps up or down, and jumps into water should be approached on a short stride with the horse's hocks well under him; straightforward obstacles, ditches, and open water should be met on a lengthening stride. If your horse tends to jump big, you may wish to approach trappy situations from a trot; however, school your horse to come back into your hand and leg at the canter so that you will be able to establish a good rhythm throughout the course.

The pace for the Pre-training level is a strong canter; for the Training, a hand gallop. Try to settle your horse into the rhythm of the pace right from the start; he should be willing to shorten his stride on turns and in trappy places and lengthen his stride in the open stretches while still maintaining a good rhythm. This will give both you and the horse confidence.

Certain types of fences always present the biggest problems and should be schooled at home, as it is unfair, and usually unsuccessful, to ask even the boldest horse to tackle them in cold blood. The first of these are jumps into water. A horse is naturally suspicious of water because he cannot see what the footing is underneath him.

Practice walking him through narrow, then wide, shallow streams that have a good gravel bottom. When he does this exercise without hesitation, trot and canter him through so that he gets accustomed to the splashing water. Then find a stream or pond one and a half to two feet deep and work through that until he learns how to use his legs in the deeper water. Next, set a low fence on the edge of shallow water that is wide enough for the horse to jump into, rather than over; school this at a trot and canter. If possible, find a stream with a bank two or three feet high and jump down into the water. School your horse through any water you can find as long as the footing is good; if you are not sure of footing, go slow. Go back to the simplest exercises if your horse ever does get a scare in the water.

Ditches, with or without water, are probably the next biggest problem to the horse because he must look down to see what he is jumping. The very act of looking down tends to stop him. Start schooling over natural, shallow ditches. Continue until your horse recognizes a ditch some strides away by its appearance and by the way you are riding him (using a strong leg, keeping your eyes and his head up) and he tackles it willingly. Then school him over a manmade ditch that is a couple of feet deep and revetted (the banks held back by boards, railroad ties, etc.), as this will have a different "look" to him.

Combinations are also an important problem, although at the lower levels they should be relatively straightforward. They come in three basic types: a double or triple vertical in-and-out on the same level; a mixture of types, such as a drop followed by a ditch followed by a jump up a bank; and finally, an arrangement of elements involving a sharp turn in order to negotiate the "out." If the distance is long between the elements, meet them on a long stride; if short, meet them on a short stride, or even trot to the first element if you can maintain enough impulsion so that the horse will not stop.

You will also find fences where you will have a choice of jumping in different ways. A simple example is the "brandy snifter." Picture a brandy snifter lying on its side; the stem may be made of two parallel logs, possibly measuring above the maximum height for the level: the bowl of the glass will be formed by two curved fences to be jumped as an in-and-out. Your choice will be made on the knowledge of your horse's ability: if he is bold and strong you would choose the "stem"; if he is cautious and the striding suits him, you would choose the "bowl." When time is important, you must give preference to the fastest way if it is possible for your horse.

A precise approach is important to the success of handling a combination or a choice fence so that the horse knows exactly where you wish to jump the obstacle and so that he has the maximum opportunity to turn if necessary. Check your rules on refusals and combinations and be sure you thoroughly understand where the penalty zones are, particularly where they overlap, so that you do not inadvertently have a technical refusal by crossing your track or leaving the penalty zone as you make a turn into an element.

THE EVENT

On the day before the event there is usually an "official" course-walking at some point in the afternoon. It is wise to go on this if at all possible as there is usually an official of the event in charge and you can then ask any questions about the course, penalty zones, etc. Even if there is no official along, you will find more experienced "eventers" that will be willing to help you. After you have done the official course-walking, go back and walk it by yourself as you will not be able to remember all the details from one walk, especially when you have been distracted by a group of people. As you walk around, take notes that you can study that evening on such factors as the landmarks that will help you keep on course, where to watch out for going off course, and details about the fences.

A helper is almost essential if you plan to compete in an event. You do not wish to leave your horse unwatched while you make a final check of the cross-country and walk the stadium course. You should also be able to relax for a while so that you are fresh for the stadium course.

Allow enough time before the dressage to work your horse to the point where he will perform at his best level. Some do better if worked early in the day, given time to relax, and then only worked a short period before the test. Others do better if they are worked just before the test.

Before you ride the cross-country, check any fences you are uncertain about or where the footing may have changed due to rain. Plan to be mounted fifteen minutes (more if the horse needs settling) before the start. Go out for a short gallop and school over a couple of fences, even if you do not think your horse needs it. You wish to tune him into the job ahead, which is very different from the dressage.

Know what speed is expected and what the time allowed is for the course. Even if time does not count, you will want to know what time you did the course in compared to the standard; this is one way to learn pace. Time yourself or ask the timer immediately after you have finished before he is busy with the next starter. If this is inconvenient, ask at the scoring center later in the day.

Ride the cross-country as you have planned it, but remain alert and flexible to conditions that may call for a change in your original plans. Do not underrate any fence, no matter how simple it may appear to you; it may look different to your horse or it may ride harder than you anticipated. Be wary of the first couple of fences, especially with a green horse; he does not wish to leave the security of the

STANDARDS FOR THE FIVE LEVELS OF HORSE TRIALS

Those Eligible	*Pre-training*	*Training*	*Preliminary*	*Intermediate*	*Advanced*
	Unrated horses. Riders any age.	Unrated horses. Riders 12 years or older.	Horses grade 3 or unrated. Riders 14 years or older.	Horses grade 2 or 3. Riders 16 years or older.	Horses grade 1 or 2. Riders 16 years or older.
Dressage	1974 AHSA Training Level, Test 1 (modified)	1974 AHSA First Level, Test 1	1974 AHSA First Level, Test 3	1974 AHSA Second Level, Test 1—Three-Day: Second Level, Test 2	1975 FEI Three-Day Event Dressage Test
Roads & Tracks Phases A & C			Total of 8,000 to 10,000 m. to be carried out at a speed of 240 m.p.m.	Total 8,000 to 16,000 m. to be carried out at a speed of 240 m.p.m.	Total of 10,000 to 16,000 m. to be carried out at a speed of 240 m.p.m.
Steeplechase			From 2,500 to 3,200 m. to be carried out at a speed of 640 m.p.m.	From 2,500 to 3,600 m. to be carried out at a speed of 640 m.p.m.	From 3,000 to 3,600 m. to be carried out at a speed of 690 m.p.m.
Solid part of obstacle shall not exceed			3′	3′3″	3′3″
Overall height of brush shall not exceed			4′7″	4′7″	4′7″
Cross-country	Not to exceed 2,400 m. carried at a speed of not more than 350 m.p.m	From 2,000 to 3,600 m. to be carried out at a speed of 400 to 450 m.p.m.	From 2,800 to 3,600 m. to be carried out at speeds of 520 m.p.m.	From 3,200 to 4,000 m. to be carried out at a speed of 550 m.p.m.	From 3,200 to 4,800 m. to be carried out at a speed of 570 m.p.m.
Number of obstacles	12–15	12–15	18–20	18–22	20–30
Solid part shall not exceed the height of	approx. 3′	3′3″	3′7″	3′9″	3′11″
Spread at highest point shall not exceed	approx. 3′6″	3′11″	4′7″	5′3″	5′11″
Spread at the base shall not exceed	approx. 4′6″	5′3″	6′7″	8′	9′2″

m.=meters
m.p.m.=meters per minute
1.00 m.=3 ft. 3.37 in.
1.00 kilometer=5/8 of a mile
1600 m.=1 mile

m.p.h.=miles per hour
240 m.p.m.=9 m.p.h
350 m.p.m.=13 m.p.h.
450 m.p.m.=16¾ m.p.h.
520 m.p.m.=19⅜ m.p.h.

CLASSIFICATION OF HORSES:

Grade 1—Horses that have completed a CCI or CCIO, or placed two times at the Advanced Level, or three times at the Intermediate Level or some combination thereof.

Grade 2—Horses that have placed two times at the Intermediate Level, or three times at the Preliminary Level or some combination thereof.

Grade 3—Horses that have completed a Three-Day Event, or placed two times at the Preliminary Level, or three times at the Training Level or some combination thereof.

All other horses are classified as Unrated. Only placing first through fifth at USCTA Approved Events are used in determining the classification of a horse.

Pre-Training tests often do not have a time allowed or a time limit.

Open Training, Open Preliminary and Open Intermediate divisions are open to horses graded one level above the stated division.

If cross-country-type obstacles, i.e., water, timber, are included in the Steeplechase, they must conform to the cross-country standards of that division.

To be eligible for Preliminary and higher competitions horses must be five years of age or older.

All fences involving height are measured from the horse's normal takeoff point.

The height and width of all stadium obstacles are regulated by the same standards as those of the cross-country for each division.

At the Advanced and Intermediate Levels only 50% of the fences may be of maximum height.

At the Preliminary and Training Levels at least ⅔ of the fences should be of maximum height; at least 20% of the obstacles at all levels should be of maximum height and spread, and at least 10% of the obstacles should be without height.

group and he has not yet had time to gather enthusiasm for the job.

The horse that is not having trouble with the course has the right of way over the horse with problems. If there is a horse in your way, call "ware horse," and they should immediately clear the area. However, if there is a horse blocking an obstacle for whatever reason, pull up *outside the penalty zone.*

Actually, an official should stop you well in advance and start taking the hold-up time with a stopwatch. When it is all right for you to go, the official should then notify you that he will take your time as you pass the point where you were stopped. You should then go well back from this point so that you have re-established the galloping rhythm and put your horse's mind back to the job by the moment you pass the timer.

Some officials say that they are going to give you a countdown of ten and then you are to start. They should not do this, but remember they are all volunteers and some are more knowledgeable than others. Simply ask them for a one-minute warning. Spend some of the time while you are waiting establishing with the timer how you are going to restart, and in the meanwhile keep your horse walking and alert.

After you have completed the last fence, do not make a mad dash for the finish. If you have not had any trouble on the course, you should not have any time penalties. If you have had a couple of refusals, you are probably out of the ribbons anyway, so save your horse's strength in order to make a good showing in the stadium jumping. The way to make time on the cross-country is to use *all* the good stretches to gallop on.

You are only allowed three refusals at any obstacle and then you must retire or go on to the next obstacle, depending on the rules of the event. Even if the fence judge does not stop you, do not try the fence again as you may impede an oncoming competitor, damage the fence, and/or tear up the footing. The likelihood of your getting over the fence after three refusals is small and there always is another day. Be a good sport and treat others as you would wish them to treat you.

If you miss the finish flags, immediately turn around and go through them. You are not disqualified but have simply lost time. Dismount and take care of your horse the same way you would after any hard work. Offer him water and hay when he is cool.

Always walk the stadium on foot a couple of times. Note where the tight turns are and where the striding in a combination may be difficult for your horse. Watch how other horses similar to yours handle the combinations in order to get an idea whether you want two short strides or one long one. Remember to salute the judges and wait for the starting bell before going through the starting flags.

If you have a fall on either the cross-country or the stadium, you must remount at the point where you fell. The clock keeps running. When you knock down a fence that must be reset, the bell will sound and you must wait for the bell to sound again before restarting. This time is taken and subtracted from the total. The dressage tests are available after the scores have been totaled. Ribbon winners are expected to present themselves mounted and in proper attire.

Combined Training is one of the most demanding of the horse sports. It gives a small return in the way of prizes and ribbons but a very large return in the way of satisfaction.

PHASES OF THE EVENT

So many forms of horsemanship and so many practical skills are demanded in a Combined Training Event that each merits discussion on its own. We have chosen to highlight several phases of Eventing which we feel riders ought to know more about.

The author and her grade gelding Aasgaard performing a circle to the left at the canter at the Sacramento Valley Dressage Show. *(Photo by Catherine McWilliams.)*

Just What Is Dressage?

By
CATHERINE McWILLIAMS

Dressage training and competition are rapidly gaining popularity in the U.S., and would probably enjoy an even larger vogue if more riders knew what dressage was all about.

Several features of this sport make it attractive to riders who are involved in schooling and showing their horses. First is the desire to ride one's own horse with the elegance and harmony that every good dressage rider exhibits. Second is a dissatisfaction with one's present level of schooling and faulty, hit-or-miss communication with one's horse. Dressage offers a way to improve not only communication and obedience, but can also improve a horse's way of going and even his conformation.

The term "dressage" is often used today in a more limited sense than it deserves. Most riders not trained in this discipline regard it as a specialized style of riding, practiced for its own sake, in a class with the specialized training for polo ponies or gaited horses. Nothing could be further from the truth: dressage, rather than a specialized offshoot of English riding, is the fundamental system on which the training of any horse should be based.

Dressage means the training of the horse in a certain poise, wherein he is responsive to the leg and weight aids of the rider, as well as being continually and softly in contact with the rider's hand through his supple acceptance of and seeking for a light rein pressure. Careful training of a horse in this poise will result in a horse obedient and cheerful in performing the requirements of classical dressage in the arena, and in being a pleasurable mount to ride on any other task. This is because the horse's mind and body are harmoniously developed to carry out the rider's demands quickly and efficiently, with a minimum of resistance and wasted effort.

Lest this description sound mysterious and impossible for ordinary mortals to achieve, keep in mind that this obedience is in reference to the simplest matters: going forward, smoothly turning right or left, stopping, changing from one gait to another. These are recognized throughout dressage training as indispensible to, and in this sense more important than, the performance of the more difficult school figures that usually come to mind when dressage is mentioned, such as the movements on two tracks, flying changes of lead, and the highly balanced gaits (passage and piaffe).

Regardless of the final purpose of the horse, he should be schooled exactly as a prospective dressage horse. If he is intended for some purpose other than dressage, his education is considered completed at a lower level of achievement, but these lower levels are the same ones that every dressage horse must pass through. For example, a true pleasure horse might only be schooled to the First or Second level (see below for explanation of the levels), a show hunter to Second or Third, and a top equitation horse or stadium jumper perhaps as high as Fourth level. A Three-Day Event horse is required to perform a dressage test as part of each event; open competition requires Third level dressage.

Competition in dressage is available at every level from the most elementary up to Olympic standard. A dressage competition requires a horse and rider to perform individually a predetermined, usually memorized, pattern of gaits, circles, halts, changes of direction, etc., in a special arena (see page 128). The arena is marked by a low (around one foot) white fencing, and measures 20 by 40 meters (66 by 132 feet) for the lower levels, and 20 by 60 meters for the higher levels. Along the boundary are large letter markers which determine where each movement begins and ends.

The tests are written by the AHSA. They range from the easiest, training level, through levels One, Two, Three, and Four, the most advanced. Above these levels are three international levels, written by the FEI, with progressively difficult requirements through Prix-St.-Georges, Intermediare, to Grand Prix, the test used in the Olympics.

The requirements of each level are carefully graded to provide in themselves an indication of how training should progress. Training level requires a horse quietly accepting contact with the bit (always a simple snaffle), and performing an ordinary walk, working trot, working canter, circles the width of the arena, and transitions between trot and halt, walk and trot, and trot and canter.

First level adds smaller circles at the trot, changes of lead through the trot, and extended trot.

Second level includes smaller canter circles, depart into canter from the walk, shoulder-in, turn on the haunches, and backing.

Third level is the first time collected gaits are required. At this level a simple double bridle becomes optional, although the plain snaffle may be used through the Fourth level, after which the double bridle is required. The requirements of Third level include ordinary and extended walk; collected, ordinary (a much more vigorous and brilliant gait than "working"), and extended forms of both trot and canter; two-track, and counter-canter (on the "wrong" lead).

The higher levels bring more and more difficult transitions between the gaits, smaller circles, single and repeated flying changes of lead, pirouettes, and ultimately, in the Grand Prix, passage, piaffe, and flying changes of lead every stride.

A dressage competition will designate which tests will be offered, and a competitor may choose any test he wishes to ride, with the fol-

The author riding her grade gelding Aasgaard over a hunter type fence. (Photo by Catherine McWilliams.)

He is equally at ease clearing the higher fences of a jumping course. (Photo by Catherine McWilliams.)

Aasgaard at the extended trot in Dressage competition. The following week he won ribbons in both hunter and jumper classes. *(Photo by Catherine McWilliams.)*

lowing restrictions: no one horse is allowed to show in more than two consecutive levels, and a horse may not compete in Training through Third level if he has already received three scores over 70 percent in that level. Each test is divided into a group of 15 or more movements or parts, each of which receives a separate score, on a scale of 0 to 10. Each ride takes several minutes, and the judge watches the entire ride, dictating his scores as well as comments on every movement to a secretary, who writes these on the competitor's test sheet, which is given to him at the end of the class. Each test, in addition to the scores on the prescribed movements, includes four scores under "General Impressions." The judge's comments on these three aspects of the horse's schooling (Obedience, Paces, and Impulsion) plus the position and seat of the rider, can be of particular value for further schooling.

The judge scores each movement against his highly educated ideal of perfection, rather than against the other horses in the class. The scores are then converted into percentages, and prizes are awarded on this basis. Some shows also award rosettes to all riders scoring over 60 percent, emphasizing the importance of the quality of the ride rather than of beating the competition. The winning score in most dressage classes now is somewhere in the 60 percenters, although many classes are still won by scores below 60 percent, and at large shows a few scores over 80 percent are sometimes seen.

Dressage training and competition offer a great deal to the participants, and they are within reach of any rider who seriously wishes to improve his horse's performance. Local dressage organizations across the U.S. sponsor hundreds of competitions and schooling shows each year, as well as meetings, lectures, clinics, and publications, and they are all eager to welcome anyone interested in learning more about this equestrian art.

Preparing for the Cross-Country

By
JACK LeGOFF

Early Schooling for Cross-Country

Start teaching your horse to jump by working over Cavalletti, first at the walk and then by trotting over them—slowly. Then school him over a variety of small fences at the trot. Schooling over low fences will build the horse's confidence. Then do the same thing at a slow canter. Remember, never force your horse over high fences as he will lose his confidence. Gradually add ditches, banks, drops and water jumps and bullfinches to the usual fences, and when your horse handles these with ease you are both ready for serious cross-country schooling.

Requirements for Cross-Country Riding

There are several requirements—the right speed, the right impulsion, the right balance and the right timing. I put timing last in cross-country, because here timing is more the work of the horse than of the rider as compared to stadium jumping.

The Importance of Correct Speed

Speed is very important. When you play a game, you have to know the rules. If you don't know what your speed can be and actually is, you will just go flat out, or too slow. The most important thing to do is to go clean, first. Horses that travel at slower speeds are less apt to get hurt, less apt to hurt their riders, less apt to come in with poor condition or attitudes for the next day's jumping test. Unnecessary speed makes horses excited and disobedient. It doesn't make any sense to go too fast or faster than is safe and good for the horse. The right speed is very important. If it is right, you are in pretty good shape.

You must not go into a fence sawing on a horse's mouth. This makes him raise his head so that he can't see the jump. He has to see where he is going and just where to put his feet. You must not mess around with your hands at this point.

The speed changes with the particular fence. A spread takes more speed. The horse needs impulsion over the fence, but not in his long approach. Don't go too fast on the flat and then go dead at the fence. Regulate the speed between the fences and go with the horse at the fence, when necessary. But remember to go in slowly if there is a slide or drop or water on the far side of the jump. Don't go into these fast. Remember, a horse can jump 2½ or 3 feet easily from a trot.

Creating Impulsion

Impulsion is the horse's desire to move forward. If your horse has impulsion, you have only to give him your hands, and the horse moves forward, your legs being close on each side of the horse. The rider regulates impulsion with his hands, but he must create it with his legs. You must have your legs on the horse all the time. Be able to feel your horse with your calves—just feel, not squeeze. You must teach your horse to accept the feel of your leg all the time, just as he was taught to accept the feel of the saddle. If you can't teach him to accept this, get another horse.

Choosing the Correct Line

Sometimes it is much better to take a corner. Pick your line early and be very precise in riding it. You should be in full control of the direction even in the air. Be a pilot, not a passenger.

Jumping Ditches, Water Jumps, and Banks

At a ditch, a water jump, or a bank, interfere as little as possible with your horse. Regulate the speed and the direction, but do not regulate the stride. On these jumps the horse must do this himself. Increase speed, but don't go with a longer stride. Ask with your legs, but hold in a shorter stride, because a shorter stride meets the right takeoff point more easily. Look at the point of takeoff line you desire. For once keep your eyes on this line in front of the jump. It will help you to keep your weight forward and your horse will be less apt to jump standing back.

Be careful at a splash not to come in too fast, as your horse will trip in the water and lose his balance.

Going up banks, stay close to the saddle with your legs and seat. Don't interfere with the stride. Going down banks, keep your legs on the girth and close them tight to straighten your back a little and keep your balance. If you sit too far back going down a bank, you will get a good buck. Stay forward as much as you can, so as not to lose your balance.

Conditioning Your Horse for Cross-Country

Get him in good condition with enough wind for a two- or three-mile course. To do this, he should be at a point where he can work for an hour on the flat without tiring. Then gallop him a mile. A week later, having worked every day or nearly every day, gallop a mile again. Never gallop more than two miles at a time. The next week after the mile gallop, give him a three- or four-minute break, then gallop again. Each week this second gallop may be longer. Gradually work this second gallop up to two miles after the 3- or 4-minute break. (A longer or shorter break will not do.) In the last three weeks gallop him every 5 days, finishing the gallop going up hill. When the horse finishes this exercise coming uphill strong, he is ready.

Gauge Your Speed

The ideal speed for roads and tracks is 240 meters per minute at a steady trot. This comes out at 1000 meters (⅔ mile) in 4 minutes.

If you are supposed to ride at 400 meters per minute to average 400 meters, go faster on straightaways and slower on turns or in less favorable areas. If you have a hot horse, work him consistently at 350 meters per minute and work him longer each time. Work a slow or lazy horse a little faster than 400 meters per minute. Remember: Letting a horse gallop as fast as he wants teaches him to go crazy, and to pull. Don't do it.

Walk the Course Three Times

Walk the cross-country course three times at least. Walk it the first time with the crowd at the official opening of the course. It will be impossible to concentrate at this time, but you should get a general idea of the course, of directions and lay of the land and such.

The second time walk it with your coach. Study the fences one by one. Study your approach: pick the best one. Pick your line: decide which line will work best. Studying how the fence is built will influence your choice of approach and how actually to jump it.

The third time, go alone. Walk out the line you will ride, as you laid it out the second trip. Have it well in mind before you start, as you will profit by walking the course just as you will ride it. This time pick out landmark trees you can head for from a distance. Know where your fences are from these landmarks and what the distances are so that you will know whether to go around a blind turn strong or in good control for a rapidly up-coming fence.

Memorize your course as you will ride it. Know it by heart.

Double Check Your Equipment

Go over your equipment thoroughly well before your ride to see that all equipment is strong and in good shape. As you head out toward the starting area, go over it all again, seeing that all the adjustments are properly made: girth, bit, boots, spurs, martingale and stick. Be sure to know your rules regarding combinations. Remember your responsibility to the team.

Most Important—Go Clean

Rules to remember in riding cross-country: Your first concern is to go clean—no falls, no refusals.

Go as fast as you can without taking any chances on falls or refusals, up to the maximum bonus, but not faster. Pick your lines and stick to them. Make nice turns. Meet your fences straight on the line you have chosen—no wobbling. Be determined, keep a cool head.

USET Three-Day Coach Jack LeGoff and Mary Simmers officiating at an event. (Photo by Lorna Forbes.)

Walking a Course

By
SALLY O'CONNOR

Walking a cross-country course is serious business. It can mean the difference between a great ride or one that's botched. Go about it carefully.

The United States Three-Day Event Team, for instance, walked the Burghley course with Jack LeGoff. They discussed each of the fences at length, walked in and out of water jumps to determine the depth and footing, measured the combinations and proposed various strategies. Then each member of the team went back alone, not just once, but at least three more times. It paid off with a big win.

Your own plan of attack should include the "Official Walking" held, usually, the day before the actual competition. One of the officials will conduct you and the other competitors around the course, pointing out any special rules or regulations and showing where mandatory markers are placed. By this time you should have a map of the cross-country course (furnished by the event organizers), so you can make notes on it as you go along—particularly on any jumps that involve complicated approaches or options. Now, too, is the time to ask questions regarding the rules. You don't want to go off-course and be eliminated. If in doubt, ask! Often the other competitors will offer advice about a particular obstacle. Try to note all that you hear and evaluate it later deciding which suggestions to adapt, and which to ignore.

The official walking, of course, is not sufficient. For one thing, nearly all of the competitors will be along. Sometimes, in fact, it's hard to see the jumps through the crowd! The chatter, too, can get in the way of a thorough examination of the fences.

You'll want to go back again, this time in the company of your coach or an experienced rider. Concentrate on the course—not just on the jumps, but on the approaches, the turns, the tricky places. Together, you and your companion should come up with a pretty good idea of how each fence will be ridden. Again, jot these things down on your map.

There's a third walk in store for you, this time alone. It will help to engrave the course in your memory so that, when you're riding and the jumps are coming up much faster, you'll know exactly where you are and what is coming up next. Some courses are very poorly marked or use wooded trails. It's often too easy to take a wrong turn. It's a good idea, then, to take note of various landmarks and to think about the fences in relation to each other. Note the halfway point, too, so you can check your time when you ride.

If you are at all worried about going off course, don't be too proud to go back again and again. Knowing the course well is half the battle.

In addition to memorizing the course itself, there are various things you should look for. Consider first the terrain. Overall, is it a good galloping course or one that will require a slower pace? What and where are the spots that call for caution? Look for places that are muddy or rocky. Moving too fast through mud will tire your horse rapidly or could cause your horse to pull a tendon. Galloping madly over rocks can give him a stone bruise or cause him to stumble. Take all of these things into account. And consider yourself, too. You don't want to knock your knees by racing along narrow wooded trails.

On the other hand, look for galloping spots where you can make up for lost time. Look for shortcuts, too. As long as there are no compulsory markers, you can take any path between two fences. By playing it smart, you can often save yourself a good bit of ground and time.

Consider the lay of the course—its twists and turns. Remember that a horse which goes along and jumps anything out hunting may not be as willing when asked to jump on his own, "in cold blood," as it were. Those first three fences, when he's asked to move away from the other horses and the trailers, must be ridden very firmly, however straightforward and simple they seem.

Keep in mind, too, that your horse is likely to pick up speed and be harder to control whenever the course loops back toward the barns and his fellow equines. Be prepared for this and don't let your horse fall into this pattern!

Now inspect each jump carefully. Most of the fences will be solid—much more so than those you've encountered at shows. They may look enormous to you, but remember, to the horse, they are inviting. If you ride them firmly, you should have no problem.

Fences that present optical illusions are the trouble spots. Seek them out and plan for them. A fence with a false ground line may confuse the horse about where to take off.

Light patterns frequently trouble horses, so take extra care when you're asked to jump from a brightly lit area into shade. A horse's eyes do not adjust readily to sudden light shifts, so expect some hesitation when approaching an obstacle set under a big shady tree.

Approaches which are cluttered will bear much study. Make sure you are riding firmly enough to get your horse to look at the fence, *not* at the clutter around or in front of it.

Remember, too, that horses will jump natural obstacles much more readily than they will painted ones. If there's a white coop on the course, for instance, note that you'll have to push harder than you might at a natural post and rail.

Water fences and ditches seem to cause a great deal of unnecessary strife. There's no use trying to introduce your horse to these in competition. What counts here is the homework you've done. If you've included these in your schooling, you are already aware of your horse's reaction to them and can ride accordingly.

If you haven't had any experience with drop fences, relax. Horses have little trouble negotiating them. Riders, unfortunately, tend to tighten up and transmit their own lack of confidence to the horse. Ride with confidence and don't look down!

Slides and banks should be inspected with care, but they rarely cause a horse to stop. Look out for roots and stumps and things that might get in your horse's way.

If the course contains any combination or option fences, be thorough in your approach to them. Stride off the distance between elements and choose the best distance for your horse's stride. You can't just barrel into a combination and leave the problem to your horse. If he's brought in badly, you might be asking him to take on an impossible distance!

With option fences, consider your horse's ability and the degree of his training. Let's say you are faced with the choice of an in-and-out, a big spread, or a simple fence with a difficult approach.

If your horse is a big, bold jumper, take the spread. If he's at all hesitant, play it safe with the in-and-out. If he jumps handily and you have no trouble restraining him, go at the simple fence with the tricky approach.

When you have to jump down into a road, cross it, and jump again on the other side, be wary. Your horse will probably want to turn off onto the track rather than jump another fence. Be ready.

Finally, don't forget about the weather. If you're walking the course the day before an event and it is likely to rain the next day, make a mental note of areas which are likely to be slick or muddy. In other words, be prepared for everything.

As you can see, a good ride in the cross-country takes more than a bit of luck. Walking the course intelligently will bring you a long way toward your goal.

The Ten Minute Break

By
MARSHALL GRAY

The importance of the care of the horse at the ten minute break during the endurance phase of the Three-Day Event and afterwards cannot be stressed enough. There are only about ten short minutes at the Vet check in which to refresh the horse as much as possible, go over all equipment, and be ready for the most difficult phase of the event—the cross-country. It is essential that the rider and groom be organized, well ahead of time, in order to work with maximum efficiency during the break.

The groom should be familiar with the layout of the Vet check area and its facilities in advance. The night before the cross-country all equipment should be laid out, double-checked and ready to go. Early next morning (well before the first horse starts), transport all equipment to the site, hopefully early enough to choose a strategic position to leave everything. This means near the water supply, in shade if hot, uphill if wet, etc. All equipment should be plainly and well marked.

The following list is meant only as a guideline, as each horse and rider situation is different:

2 large, light wash buckets
1 bucket for drinking water only
Small sponge for rinsing out mouth
Large body sponge, and scraper
Body wash with camphor added to wash water to insure quick evaporation
Ice, if weather is hot
Containers for carrying water if supply

is not readily available, or for bringing in warm water if weather is cold
Extra tack: bridle, stirrup leather, girth, halter and shank, martingale, breastplate, boots, etc.
Towels
Sweat sheet, cooler (depending on weather) surcingle
Rain sheets—even if it's not raining they are handy to set up a dry, neat "shop"
Extra set of horse's shoes: studs, if used
Shoe removal tools (better to go without, than with a twisted shoe if the farrier is not available)

Emergency First-Aid:
- Instant ice packs
- Sheet cotton
- Gauze sponges
- Antiseptic
- Scissors
- 1″ and ½″ adhesive tape
- 4″ Elastoplast (Elastikon doesn't stick well if wet)
- Spider bandages, flannel wrap, pins, sponge
- Non-adherent dressing
- 4″ self-adherent soft gauze wrap
- Pencil and paper

All of the above, plus odds and ends, can fit neatly into a fishing or tool box without the tray. Also:
Salt tablets and water or soft drink for rider
Rider's personal things, i.e., gloves, etc.

The groom must be in the Box to meet the rider at the end of Phase C, with all equipment ready and waiting. As the rider dismounts, the groom puts on the horse's halter, loosens (does not undo) the noseband, runs up the stirrups, undoes the overgirth, loosens the girth, and then starts walking the horse slowly, at the same time checking legs and shoes for any major wrong.

After one or two turns, the groom removes the horse's boots, dunks them in the water bucket if there is any dirt on the inside, and checks the legs very carefully. The groom should then start washing the horse. If the weather is hot, lots of cool water should be used, primarily sponging it on the head, throat, chest, and between the hind legs and dock. Then the horse should be walked again for a couple of turns, repeating the previous procedure, as necessary. The amount of water used depends on the weather. Studs should be changed if required.

If the weather is very hot, ice can be used to help cool the horse during the washing procedure. It can be applied to the throat, head, and between the front legs and dock areas, which will help reduce the horse's temperature. Do *not* put ice on the major muscle areas such as the neck, back, or hindquarters as this will stiffen these muscles. Be sure to walk the horse in the coolest area possible, in the shade, where the air is moving.

If the weather is cold or windy, select a protected area in which to walk the horse. If it is raining, it is usually better not to use the rain sheet, as the horse will only steam under it and get hotter.

By now, there will be about five minutes left. Now remove excess water from the legs and replace the boots, if used. With the four-minute warning, the horse should be tacked up, saddle reset, etc. While it is the rider's responsibility to be sure all equipment is exactly in order and fitted properly, the groom should know just what the rider expects!

At the two-minute warning, the rider mounts, tightens the girths, and makes a last minute check to see that all is in order.

Once the rider is on course, the groom should tidy up the area, replenish the water supply and take the necessary equipment to the weigh-out area at the end of the cross-country. There the groom should wait at the scales to take the horse once it is released from the official horse holder. It is very important to be familiar with "un-authorized assistance" rules, so as not to unwittingly eliminate the rider! Depending on circumstances, the horse can be cooled out completely there (following basically the previous procedure) or led almost directly back to the stable if nearby, and cooled out and cared for there.

Once the event is over, all equipment should be collected as soon as possible. The rider's friends or relatives can be most helpful in this situation.

Please remember that all of this is intended only as a guideline. There are no hard and fast procedures that can be set up. Every event will differ, generally because of the weather, as frequently last minute or unforeseen situations arise, and the groom must be ready to react accordingly.

TRAINING ADVICE FROM THE EXPERTS

Jimmy Wofford, two-time Olympic competitor, on Clodomir. *(Photo by Alix Coleman.)*

Conditioning the Horse for the Preliminary Level Three-Day Event

By
JIMMY WOFFORD

Eventers in the greatest need of a conditioning program are those at the Preliminary level. While more advanced competitors have their experience to draw on, beginners have no such guide and are apt to finish an event with an exhausted or distressed horse because of an inadequate fitness program. The program suggested here is based on Interval Training and is designed to prepare a horse properly for Eventing.

Many conditioning programs can produce a horse "fit" enough to cross the finish line with still a little to spare. One finds these conditioning programs mainly at the higher levels of eventing where the rider has had the benefit of ample knowledge acquired from years of exposure. This situation, however, is not the case at the Preliminary Level where riders simply do not know how to condition their horses and therefore must devise their own hit-or-miss system, with frequently less than adequate results. It is for these riders, and for those who are moving their horses up into the Three-Day sphere for the first time, that I have set forth this "schedule."

Interval Training has proven to increase the endurance performances of human as well as equine athletes. Galloping the horse for short intervals, as opposed to other methods of long conditioning gallops (for as long as an hour in some cases), has resulted in less wear on legs and feet: in short, in generally sounder horses for a longer period of time.

Now, before we launch into this conditioning schedule, I would like to emphasize that it is only intended as a guide, and not an ironclad rule. Each horse is an individual and must be trained accordingly. There are many variables to be taken into consideration, such as age, condition, temperament and soundness of the horse. But because there is a need for some sort of program to help riders condition their horses with minimum stress, one must start somewhere. The "general" schedule should be used with flexibility in mind.

There are several important factors which must be considered before starting the Interval Training schedule. The horse must have:

1. Competed at the Preliminary One-Day Event Level with satisfactory results.
2. Had no lameness or lingering illness.
3. Been wormed within the last 60 days.
4. Had his teeth floated within the last 60 days.
5. Had a current blood chemistry report, with a red blood cell count of better than 35, and a hemoglobin of better than 12, or be on a program to correct any deficiencies.
6. Regularly been cleaning up a balanced meal; fed at least three times a day, with amounts suitable for the horse's size and temperament.
7. Been in steady work for at least 60 days and be capable of 1½ hours of hacking at the walk and trot over rolling terrain.

There are a few general areas that I would like to elaborate on which might be helpful while working with the conditioning program:

KEEP A DIARY—insure that your work is logical and progressive.

WALK—when the schedule calls for "walk" this does not mean idling along "on the buckle." The walk should be energetic and lively, and the horse should be on the bit most of the time, using himself.

DRESSAGE—do your work little and often. Plan your work so that your horse warms up gradually, moves on to his most difficult movements and transitions, then end the period doing the movements he does the best and enjoys the most. Never end the work period on a bad note.

CAVALETTI—most of the time there is no need to school over 3′. Instead, strive for style, cadence and self-carriage. If your horse quickens or steps, don't get excited. Analyze the reasons and deal with them in a logical fashion. Practice maintaining your composure, so that a calm, methodical approach becomes second nature to you. If you lose your head at home, you will lose your ribbon at the event.

HACKING—vary your route as much as possible, to keep your horse's attitude fresh.

CANTERS AND GALLOPS—do them under the same conditions throughout the training cycle, in order to cut down on the variables involved, such as temperature, footing and terrain.

TRAIN YOUR INDIVIDUAL HORSE—don't train mechanically. If your horse is cold-blooded and sluggish, add more fast work in the later stages of the training. If he is hot-blooded, use fewer longer cantering sets, and try to get him to settle in his work.

TURN YOUR HORSE OUT—if you have the facilities. Turning out and long walks are your best defense against horses that get an edge too soon.

SCHOOLING OVER SHOW JUMPS—once you start don't worry about timing your horse's stride. Give him the correct direction and impulsion, and make him do the rest. If you make him dependent on you now, you will be in real trouble on cross-country day.

HORSE'S INDIVIDUAL PATTERN—keep this in mind when doing your pulse and respiration ratios. His own pattern is more important than some statistical average.

CHANGES—be alert to any change in your horse's attitude, his appetite, coat, droppings, appearance, muscle tone or anything else, no matter how small. You have to train the whole horse, so that he arrives on Dressage day in perfect mental and physical condition.

EXERCISE YOURSELF—be sure that you will be as fit as your horse. Riding only one horse a day *won't* be enough.

NEVER OVERLOOK ANY DETAIL—no matter how small or large. There is no such thing as "too much trouble" for an eventer.

PULSE AND RESPIRATION RATIOS

The horse's average pulse is 38–45 per minute at rest.

The horse's average respiration is 10–14 per minute at rest.

This gives you a 4 to 1 ratio at rest.

With this in mind, and knowing your own horse's pattern, dismount immediately after *completing* your gallops, take his pulse and respiration (P/R) ratio and record this figure. Then walk him in hand for ten minutes and take it again. Record this second figure, then cool your horse out. Compare these figures with those from the next work and be alert for changes.

Examine your horse's pattern with the following parameters in mind:

1. The total of the Pulse and Respiration should never exceed 180 or the horse is exhausted. This total should drop 30% within 10 minutes.
2. If the pulse exceeds 100 and has not dropped at least 20% within 10 minutes, the horse is exhausted. The same applies to the respiration figures.
3. If the respiration exceeds the pulse, the horse is exhausted.
4. The horse's maximum effective pulse rate is about 120. To achieve an improvement in your horse's capacity, the pulse should rise to 60% of maximum.
5. Always remember that the numbers will change with each horse. It is the pattern which is of paramount importance.

TRAINING SCHEDULE

The Preliminary Three-Day horse should plan to train generally along the following lines during the last three-month training period:

March

25 1½ hours at a walk over rolling countryside, utilizing hills to the best advantage—jog up hills a total of 15 minutes.

26 Hack about ½ hour, then trot 5 minutes at 240 mpm,* walk 2-3 minutes; canter 4 mins. (1600 meters) at 400 mpm. Take Pulse and Respiration ratio.

27 1 hour of walking, plus 15 minutes of Dressage.

28 Schooling over Cavaletti.

29 1½ hours at walk, plus 30 minutes of Dressage.

30 Dressage show, or local Hunter show. If none available, school over show jumps; ride a few courses.

31 Rest day—hand walk, and graze or turn out.

* *The 2-3 min. walk is the interval of rest that is given the horse between each repetition (thus the term "Interval Training"). Vary the length of the interval according to the degree of difficulty, but* Never Exceed Three Minutes. *After each final gallop, take Pulse and Respiration ratio.*

April

1 1½ hours at walk over rolling country and hills—jog up hills total of 15 minutes.

2 School over Cavaletti.

3 Hack about ½ hour then trot 5 mins. 240 mpm.; walk 2-3 mins.; trot 5 mins. 240 mpm.; walk 2-3 mins.; canter 4 mins. (1600 meters) at 400 mpm.; walk 2-3 mins.; twice. *(There is always a period of rest [walk] between every trot and canter.)* Take pulse and respiration ratio.

4 1 hour walk.

5 1 hour—hills plus 30 minutes of Dressage.

6 Dressage show or local Hunter show or school a course.

7 Rest day—hand walk and graze.

8 2 hours—rolling country and hills, jog up hills, total of 15 minutes.

9 School—Cavaletti.

10 Hack ½ hour, then trot 5 minutes at 240 mpm three times; canter 4 mins. (1600

meters) at 400 mpm three times. Take pulse and respiration ratio.
11 1½ hours—walk.
12 1 hour walk plus practice Dressage ride.
13 Schooling—Cross-country, 1600 meters to 2000 meters over a 3′ course.
14 Rest day—hand walk and graze.
15 2 hours—rolling country and hills, 15 mins., jog up hills.
16 Hack ½ hour, trot 5 mins. at 240 mpm 3 times; canter 4 mins. (1600) at 400 mpm.; canter 6 mins (2400 m) at 400 mpm.; canter 4 mins. (1600 m) at 400 mpm. Take P/R ratio.
17 1 hour walk plus 30 minutes of Dressage.
18 School—Cavaletti
19 1 hour walk plus 30 minutes of Dressage.
20 Local schooling show—do several 3′ and 3′6″ courses.
21 Rest day—hand walk and graze.
22 2 hours—rolling country and hills.
23 Hack ½ hour, trot 5 mins. at 240 mpm four times; canter 4 mins. (1600 m) at 400 mpm; 6 mins. (2400 m) at 400 mpm; 6 mins. (2400 m) at 400 mpm. Take P/R ratio.
24 1 hour walk plus 30 minutes of Dressage.
25 School—Cavaletti
26 1 hour walk plus practice dressage ride.
27 Hack about ½ hour. Trot 5 mins. at 240 mpm four times. Canter 4 mins. (1600 m) at 400 mpm; 8 mins. (3200 m) at 400 mpm; 6 mins. (2400 m) at 400 mpm. Take P/R ratio.
28 Rest day—hand walk and graze.
29 2 hours—rolling country and hills, jog up hills 30 minutes.
30 1 hour "roads" (walk and jog on *level* footing; at least 15 mins. jogging) plus 30 minutes Dressage.

May

1 Show-jump individual fences.
2 1 hour walk, plus 30 minutes Dressage.
3 Ship to Event.
4 Two-Day Event.
5 Event. If unable to go to event, ride Dressage Test and school at Preliminary speed over cross-country jumps.
6 15 minutes hand walk, morning and afternoon.
7 45 minute walk.
8 1 hour walk, plus 30 minutes of Dressage.
9 School—Cavaletti
10 Ship to Event.
11 Preliminary One-Day Event
12 Preliminary One-Day Event
13 15 minutes hand walk, morning and afternoon.
14 45 minute walk.
15 1 hour walk.
16 1 hour walk.
17 2 hours—rolling country and hills—jog uphill total of ½ hr.
18 1 hour walk, plus 30 minutes Dressage.
19 Show jump—3′3″ course.
20 Hack ½ hour. Trot 5 mins. at 240 mpm four times; canter 4 mins. (1600 m) at 400 mpm; 6 mins. (2400 m) at 400 mpm; 6 mins. at 400-500 mpm.* Take P/R ratio.
21 1 hour walk.
22 1 hour walk plus 30 minutes of Dressage.
23 School—Cavaletti.
24 1 hour walk plus 30 minutes of Dressage.
25 Hack ½ hour. Trot 5 mins. at 240 mpm four times; canter 4 mins. (1600 m) at 400 mpm.; 6 mins. (2400 m) at 400 mpm; 6 mins. at 400-500 mpm.* Take P/R ratio.
26 2 hour walk.
27 1 hour walk, plus 30 minutes of Dressage.
28 2 hours "roads" (walk and jog on *level* footing; at least 15 minutes jogging).
29 School—Cavaletti and individual show jumps.
30 1 hour hack, plus 30 minutes Dressage.
31 Ship to Event.

* *Depending on horse—keen horses slower, passive horses faster.*

June

1 Preliminary Two-Day Event
2 Preliminary Two-Day Event
3 15 minute hand walk, morning and afternoon.

4 1 hour walk.
5 1 hour walk.
6 2 hours—rolling country and hills.
7 1 hour "roads" plus 30 minutes of Dressage.
8 45 minutes of Dressage, plus Cavaletti work.
9 1½ hours "roads"—hard trotting.
10 8 mins. at 240; 2 fences, 800 meters at 550 mpm; 2 fences at 650 mpm. Take P/R ratio.
11 1 hour walk.
12 2 hours—rolling country and hills.
13 Show jump—3′9″ course.
14 45 minutes of Dressage, plus 1 hour walk.
15 Hack ½ hour; 8 mins. at 240 mpm; 6 mins. at 550 mpm; 800 meters at 800 mpm; 45 min. hack. Take P/R ratio.
16 1 hour walk.
17 Show jump—individual fences.
18 Practice Dressage movements.
19 Ship to Event.
20 Work horse, 45 mins. to 1½ hours.
21 Three-Day Event.
22 Three-Day Event.
23 Three-Day Event.

With Interval Training one can first work up to the speed required over a period of six or seven weeks, using the formula D.R.I.A. constant, V variable. Then, during the last six weeks before an event, one prepares the horse to go the required distance at this speed, using the formula D.V.I.A. constant, with R variable. Speed and distance are kept constant, with the distance kept down to 600 meters (less than half a mile), but repetitions are gradually increased up to nine or more. Interval Training should be carried out only twice a week, the other days being used for a continuation of slow work over varied terrain, as well as jumping and Dressage.

At first, a system of conditioning which involves formulae, time calculations, heart rates, etc., may sound terribly complicated. And indeed, it is no easy alternative to the more traditional methods, but Interval Training is much simpler in practice than it appears in writing and it may, in time, lead to improvements in performance better than anything yet attained in Three-Day competition. It has already done so with human athletes—it is the system which enabled long distance runners to break the four minute mile, and many feel that the phenomenal improvement in human athletic endurance performances over the past 15 years has been due largely to the development and application of Interval Training. So perhaps the time is coming when horsemen, too, may want to consider its study and development in their field. If you are interested in reading a more detailed account of Interval Training, I would suggest Noel Jackson's excellent book, *Effective Horsemanship*.

Bibliography—

Effective Horsemanship, Noel Jackson, D., Arco Publishing Co., Inc., 1968.

The Horse Trials Story, Lt. Col. C.E.G. Hope, Pelham Books Ltd., 1969.

A Cross-Country Primer

By
E. RUSSELL GOODALE

It's Tempting!

Have your ever ridden your horse over an obstacle in the open at a speed of 25 mph or thereabouts? If you have, you will probably agree with me that it was a thrill, right? The breeze smacked you in the face and brought tears to your eyes. You could feel the exhilaration, power and quickened rhythm of the horse as it bounded forward. And, as it bore down upon the obstacle, you had a fleeting wave of apprehension, almost of fear, as you thought, "Will he make it? It looks high!" And suddenly he was over with amazing ease. You couldn't help but be proud of him and, at the same time, grateful for the safe journey. Perhaps he showed you that he was proud, too, by shaking his head playfully as you galloped on.

Whether you are already a dedicated eventer, or are contemplating a career in this singular sport, you should, for your own safety and that of your horse, give particular attention to the techniques involved in salvaging obstacles at speed.

Accidents Are Usually the Fault of the Rider

I am glad to be able to say that accidents are not as frequent now as they were a few years ago, due to improved coaching, more clinics and better training opportunities. However, even one such accident is one too many; as when a horse, urged on by its rider while running the steeplechase, hurls itself through the solid part of the brush fence without even attempting to jump! The cause? Poor riding! The rider either stayed forward and kept on hand-riding right through the jump, or "threw his horse away." Either fault can result in a concussion for the rider and physical damage to the horse. Even if serious injury is avoided, the horse is left with deep psychological scars, which could affect its performance for a long time to come.

Three-Day Event

The Three-Day Event is composed of three tests usually held on three consecutive days, and includes: 1) a dressage test; 2) a speed and endurance test, composed of four phases, as follows: Phases A and C—roads and tracks; Phase B—steeplechase; Phase D—cross-country; and 3) a jumping test.

Each Test Requires a Different Seat

Eventing is like no other horse activity. It consists of three very specialized disciplines, basically very different in character and calling for different attitudes and techniques. The rider employs three types of "seat," each of which is designed to control, guide and support the movements peculiar to each discipline.

First, let's clarify the term, "seat." We say that so-and-so has a good seat, or an excellent jump seat. We are actually referring to the manner in which he manipulates his whole body. A "seat" is many things. It is poise, stability, balance, posture, flexibility, positioning of weight and muscular and reflex action. It is the principal medium of communication with the horse. A *passive* seat is "with" the horse. An *active* seat communicates to the horse its next move, change, or course of action. A proper seat is sometimes forward, sometimes back, depending upon the situation, conditions and objectives. Normally, it belongs over the center of gravity of the horse (passive seat).

Usually, the novice rider's first experience with jumping is in a ring, where his horse is necessarily limited to a moderate pace of 10 to 13 mph between jumps. Our equestrian may then broaden his experience by joining a Pony Club, or a hunt. Quite naturally, then, he or she uses the same "seat" over jumps across country as he did in the ring. Without the restraint of an enclosure, the tendency of the horse is to quicken its pace and approach a fence at a gallop instead of a canter. In place of using its back in a bascule, as it did in the ring, it takes off farther back and assumes a parabolic trajectory over the obstacle. This change of pace and style calls for a different "seat." I call it the "Steeplechase Jump Seat." The mechanics of this seat will be explained later.

Speed Needed to Win at Higher Levels

By the time you have reached the Preliminary Level, you may begin to reap the benefits of having learned to jump at speed safely and properly, for you will discover that unless you and your horse can sustain an average speed of 520 meters per minute in Phase D, you will incur penalty points which will directly affect your overall placement. In other words, the leader in cross-country usually places near the top on the score sheet. Speed is even more important at the Intermediate and Advanced Levels, where the limits of endurance and capability are approached.

Speed Requirements at the Preliminary Level

Let's look at the speeds and distances required for the test in the open at the Preliminary Level of Three-Day Events sanctioned by the United States Combined Training Association.

Phases A and C—a total of 8000 to 10,000 meters, to be carried out at a speed of 240 meters per minute, or *9 miles per hour*.

Phase B—from 2500 to 3200 meters, to be carried out at a speed of 640 meters per minute, or *23⅞ miles per hour*.

Phase D—from 4000 to 4800 meters, to be carried out at a speed of 520 meters per minute, or *19⅜ miles per hour*.

In Phase B, given a distance of 2500 meters (1.55 miles), in order to achieve an average speed of 640 meters per minute and equal the Time Required, you must cover the 2500 meters in 3 minutes, 55 seconds.

In Phase D, given a distance of 4800 meters

(3 miles), in order to achieve an average speed of 520 meters per minute and equal the Time Required, you must cover the 4800 meters in 9 minutes, 14 seconds. *Note: the Time Required is calculated by dividing the chosen distance by the chosen speed.*

Penalties

Phases A and C—One penalty point for each second in excess of the Time Required up to the time limit, which is $\frac{1}{15}$ more than the Time Required. Exceeding the time limit involves elimination.

Phase B—$\frac{8}{10}$ of a penalty point for each second in excess of the Time Required, up to the time limit, which is twice the Time Required. Exceeding the time limits means elimination.

Phase D—$\frac{4}{10}$ of a penalty point for each second in excess of the Time Required, up to the time limit, which corresponds at a speed limit of 225 meters per minute. Exceeding the time limit results in elimination.

Success in Eventing Means Hard Work

Don't expect an easy road to success in eventing. Too often, in other kinds of horse shows, blue ribbons are the result of hiring a good professional trainer to deliver Beauty to Missy at the in-gate "in-hand" and ready to attract the eyes of the judge.

But not so in eventing! You will be pretty much "on your own," because you and your horse are a team and no one else can take your place in the saddle. You must prepare him and yourself by working him daily and by fostering a relationship of mutual trust and interdependence, usually with the aid of a competent coach or instructor.

If you are eligible, join a Pony Club. If you are too old for Pony Clubbing, get yourself a good instructor and a good textbook. Learn by reading and learn by doing. Some of the greatest lessons have been learned by making mistakes, so you mustn't let the possibility of failure deter you.

Training and practice are indeed essential, but do not wait too long to enter a combined training event. One competitive effort in unfamiliar surroundings does more to educate and sharpen both horse and rider than months of practice at home. Be sure to pick an event which offers the lowest level for which you are eligible. It will be less traumatic for horse and rider.

If you are considering taking up eventing as a form of recreation, let me caution you to first count the cost. Eventing is serious business. It not only involves long hours of rigorous preparation, but it also means mental and physical strain for both horse and rider. Whenever you ride, you must *never* be just a passenger. You must be communicating with your teammate, your horse, at every step with your entire body and often with your voice. You must learn to control his every step and every move. This will require intense concentration on your part and will result as well in teaching your horse to depend completely upon you and to concentrate fully on carrying out your directives, without being distracted by other sights and sounds. Believe it or not, the horse that receives continual direction from its rider is much happier and more relaxed and will show less strain under pressure.

A Look at the International Scene

To give you some perspective, let me cite just a few of the things an international rider can make his horse do when occasion demands: 1) He tells his horse when to jump and where to take off; 2) He is able to produce an elevated, bouncy gallop in the approach to an obstacle with height; 3) He determines and sets the cadence and rhythm of his horse's movements; 4) He shortens or lengthens his horse's stride when necessary, as when approaching an obstacle or hazard; 5) He establishes his mount's gait and pace; 6) He can produce a long ground-eating stride across open country; 7) He can make his horse sprint when needed; for example, when approaching an obstacle without height, such as a water jump, or wide ditch.

U.S. Pony Club

The United States Pony Club offers an excellent opportunity to young horsemen and women to prepare for later participation in combined training events by teaching the basics of the three phases in simplified form, consisting of an obedience test, riding in the open over an outside course and negotiating simple jumps in a ring. Children are under the supervision of instructors appointed by District Commissioners.

At this stage of training it is by no means too early to lay the ground work for future demands of increased pace over obstacles. In fact, this can be accomplished progressively in early training and will result in educating the horse as well. So let's not wait to learn our ABCs in high school.

In the obedience test the young rider conducts his mount over a prescribed course, within a small ring. The routine consists of riding straight lines, turns, figure eights and serpentines, with assorted variations of walk, trot and canter as called for. Along with proper body controls, the young rider learns rein effects and how to maintain contact with the horse's mouth.

This ability to ride on contact, once learned in the obedience test within the confines of a ring, should become a permanent feature of the rider's communication with his mount. Riding cross-country, hunting, jumping, showing—whatever he does, his instructor should progressively develop and encourage the habit on the part of his pupil to ride and jump *on contact*. This is the foundation from which evolves the steeplechase jump seat!

Riding on contact with a passive hand consists of following the movements of the horse's head. To maintain contact over a jump, three movements of the rider's hands are involved, to wit: 1) at the liftoff, take with the reins; 2) suspended over the obstacle, give generously with the reins to accommodate the extension of the horse's body; and 3) upon landing, take with the reins again and follow the oscillations of the horse's head as it canters on.

These are the same movements that will be required later on in eventing, when speed becomes a factor. Here the hands are passive, or following. Gradually, as speed is increased, the hand will become more active and take a firmer hold, as the horse learns to depend upon the rider through constant communication with body, legs, weight, seat and rein effects. In this manner, with the help of good coaching, the foundation can be laid even while learning to ride, with the result that the transition to higher levels of competition will be painless.

Considerations

Now let's get technical and analyze what a horse has to do to get over an obstacle with height while traveling at a full gallop and, secondly, how the rider directs, aids and supports the horse prior to and during the three phases of the jump.

Actions of the Horse

The difficulty of jumping over a barrier from a full gallop lies in the fact that the horse's body is lengthened out and much of its weight is being carried on the forehand. The horse's balance is forward and the hindquarters are lightened in order to provide forward thrust and propel the mass forward. We say that the horse is "flattened out." And *it is impossible for a horse to raise its mass from a flattened out position!*

Consequently, before reaching the barrier, in order to raise the mass several feet above the ground without breaking the rhythm of its stride or perceptibly losing speed, it must gather itself, that is, shorten or contract the mass, at the same time shifting its center of gravity toward the rear to lighten the forehand and thus be enabled to spring upward and clear the obstacle (first phase of the jump). In flight, the body is again extended (second phase of the jump). As it lands beyond the jump, the mass is again contracted, aided by the pull of gravity. As the forehand lands first, the forward momentum is slowed momentarily, enabling the hindquarters to catch up and to place themselves well forward to provide the thrust needed to resume speed on the flat (third phase of the jump). The mass again extends in powerful leaps and is propelled toward the next obstacle.

Actions of the Rider

In these displacements of the horse's center of gravity, the rider has a very important function. Not only must he refrain from interfering with the balance and form of his mount, but he must *take direct action to help* his horse perform the difficult and precise movements described above.

How does he do this? He aids by following a basic pattern of three steps: 1) Gets ready for the jump by shifting his own weight to the rear in advance; 2) Calls the horse with a series of half-halts; and 3) Gives firm support to the horse's mouth during the approach and throughout the jump.

These aids should begin at least three strides prior to the takeoff. Up to this point the rider has assumed a forward attitude, preferably in a half-seat, maintaining contact by following the natural movements of a galloping horse. He now shifts his weight toward the rear. This can be accomplished in more than one way. He may return to the saddle and straighten his body by sitting upright. Most professional brush and timber race-riders remain up out of the saddle and shift their buttocks to the rear, leaving the upper body still inclined forward to maintain balance. The feet also remain forward in the stirrups, with the heels well down. At each of the three strides prior to the jump, he calls or signals the horse with a half-halt. In other words, he takes with the reins at each stride and simultaneously exerts pressure with back and legs in rhythm with each stride. The horse is thus alerted to the jump, and responds by gathering itself. Meanwhile, the rider braces against the stirrups, so that he can take firm hold of the reins and support the horse on the bit during the three phases of the jump. Once the horse is back on the ground, the rider may again assume a forward attitude, maintaining the necessary pace by hand-riding.

In Case of Trouble

If the horse does get into trouble during the jump, it may need instant freedom of its head to avoid a fall or accident. For example, the horse may try to "peck" to keep from falling forward. It uses its nose as a crutch by placing it on the ground for support in order to regain its balance. So be prepared to surrender your firm hold of the reins when this happens. It can save you from being pulled forward out of the saddle and perhaps landing on the ground.

A Drop Fence Demands Special Care (and Position)

A drop fence is a barrier followed by a drop of from 1.60 to 2.00 meters on the landing side. The fence may be at the top of a slope, or bank; or, as is often the case, it may be followed by a drop into water.

Undoubtedly you have seen published photographs of this type of obstacle being jumped by leading riders of the U.S. and by other international stars, such as H.R.H. Princess Anne. If the photo was snapped just as the forehand reached the landing (water or slope), you will have noticed that the rider is standing in the stirrups with the feet and legs well forward and with the upper body in a straight line, appearing as though it is almost touching the horse's rump, while the rider's hands are grasping the reins in a tight grip, in order to support the horse in maintaining its balance.

Added to the inertia caused by the forward momentum of the mass, is the force of gravity resulting from the drop of the mass. Both these forces tend to keep the horse from righting itself (that is, bringing its quarters back to a horizontal plane), which it necessarily must do to regain balance. In addition, if the landing is into water, the braking effect of the water must be taken into consideration. All these factors affect the horse's balance and make the rider's task a critical one involving strong physical action and precise judgment. The rider must use extreme care in the approach to a drop fence with regard to pace. The pace must be slow enough to avoid trouble, but not slow enough to invite a stop.

Exceptions to the Rule

I do not dispute the fact that there are and have been Three-Day Event horses of exceptional ability who know how to handle an obstacle at speed without apparent help from their riders. However, more often than not, these individuals break stride and jump off their hocks, thereby losing time at each fence. Yes, there are exceptions to every rule, but in this case the odds are rather high against finding such an animal, so I suggest that your best bet is to master the techniques involved and train your horse to hold stride and save precious time where time counts.

Happy eventing!

Ditches in a Day

By
FIFI COLES

Lorna Sutherland is an outstanding International competitor in the Three-Day Event. During a visit to the United States from Scotland, a casual conversation between Miss Sutherland and USCTA News *editor Fifi Coles produced this interview and disclosed a unique method of schooling young horses over ditches.*

It is little wonder that Britain has come to reign supreme in the sport of Three-Day Eventing. It is due in no small part to their keen sense of organization and their enormous success in competition. Badminton Horse Trials alone draws almost 100 entries which are all at the Advanced level of competition! As a result, the British have produced an outstanding number of horses and riders of very high caliber. One such rider is Lorna Sutherland who in the past several years has earned the reputation of being a consistent and courageous International competitor. Lorna, with the exception of a couple of weeks of coaching each year from Captain Eddy Goldman, works wholly on her own, schooling her horses over the few natural obstacles she can find in the countryside plus a limited number of fences she has built herself at her home in Aberdeenshire, Scotland.

Hunting, which many of the British swear by as an infallible part of an event horse's basic training, is unavailable to her geographically. Consequently, for her to continue her horses' schooling, she must travel hundreds of miles south to the heart of the eventing country. Here she stays for weeks on end in order to compete in the Novice (same as our Preliminary) Horse Trials circuit. In so doing she has produced six top event horses.

A rider of astonishing stamina, Lorna performed a feat unparalleled by any other girl by riding three horses all in the same day at Badminton where she jumped 140 obstacles on the cross-country while covering a total of 51 miles with 4-½ hours in the saddle, allowing herself only two fifteen-minute breaks between horses. After finishing in the money with two of her horses she continued, undaunted, to dance that evening until two in the morning.

When she visited the United States, I asked her about schooling young horses over ditches.

QUESTION: Ditches always seem to pose a real problem for the green horse. To riders they are often a psychological hazard. Since you have jumped just about every kind of ditch or ditch combination on two continents, what have you found to be the most successful means of solving the ditch problem?

ANSWER: My personal feeling on ditches is that it is a problem that has to be dealt with in one day. Before I start jumping ditches on any horse I am training, the horse should be jumping small timber fences, small natural fences out in the country, little stone walls and maybe colored fences at home. He should be confident and happy in his work. Then he is ready to tackle the first ditch.

If it's possible, find an area with a whole lot of ditches varying in size so that you can move from one to another. Start off with a nice small straightforward ditch. Give him a lead with another horse who jumps ditches confidently—nice and slowly. Give your horse a chance to see what he is doing, but approach the ditch with enough impulsion and speed to encourage him to jump the ditch while following the other horse. If you have no problems at this ditch, you then move on to a slightly bigger one, again with a lead. Repeat the ditches, both with a lead and then on his own. Just make a big fuss over the horse—and you will probably have no further problems with ditches.

However, to stop, even though he's been given a lead, is a normal reaction for a horse—and this is where the problem starts. If your horse absolutely will not follow the other horse over, then you might just as well send that other horse home and stay there on your own until he jumps that ditch. Now this can involve many hours sitting on the edge of that ditch. Unfortunately, at this stage you have to be a little hard on the horse. You have to insist that he jump it and you may have to hit him a couple of times and really give him the message that he's got to go over—but you must do it. Once you've got him over the ditch, you must repeat it several times until the horse jumps it fluently, and in his stride, and maintains the same speed in which he approaches the ditch. He must not put on the brakes in front of the ditch and then jump it from a standstill.

Once he's jumped a small ditch fluently in both directions, then proceed to a slightly bigger ditch with or without water (it doesn't matter) and then go on and on. However, you must not overface the horse by giving him something unjumpable. On the other hand, go on gradually, both in size of ditch and difficulty, until by the end of the session the horse is pulling into a strange ditch that he's never seen before.

He must eventually discover that a) ditches themselves don't hurt him, b) it does hurt him, by being uncomfortable, for him to stop at ditches, because you make it so. The eventual answer in his mind is: If I go I get rewarded, and it's easy. My stride will carry me over. I don't have to make a great effort. If I stop, I get punished. A horse is an animal of association. He doesn't really reason things out, but he can remember things and associate one thing with another.

Q: Do you find the approach at the canter or the trot most suitable?

A: My approach is usually at the canter. However, it depends on where your ditch is. If it's in the middle of a clean field, the canter is fine, but if the only ditches you can find are in a wooded area that is trappy, then the most suitable speed for the approach might be the trot. It gives a horse plenty of time to look at this fence, see what he's going to do, sort his feet out, and jump it.

Q: Some horses, upon catching sight of the

ditch yards away, plant their feet and just won't budge an inch further. How do you handle that?

A: One horse I was training was just such a horse. He was absolutely petrified of ditches and wouldn't go within fifteen yards of them at first. It took me three quarters of an hour to get him over his first ditch. But by the end of the day he was jumping good-sized ditches and was pulling to get at them. The thing to do is just sit at whatever point he's got to and keep at him gently with your spurs, your whip and voice. Encourage him. If he's genuinely frightened and doesn't even want to go near it, make a big fuss over him each step he takes. But—and this is important—don't let him off with going a step backwards. When eventually he makes the plunge, make a real fuss over him—and then repeat it. A normal-sized ditch, afterall, isn't as big as a horse's normal-sized stride. All you have to do is to persuade him that it's safe and more comfortable for him to go over it than it is to stay on the takeoff side.

Q: Would you ever dismount and attempt to lead him up to and over the ditch?

A: No, because it's terribly difficult. I mean a horse is ten times bigger than you are, and if he resists, you haven't a hope of pulling him over. Whereas if you're on his back and are continually agitating him, though not nastily, he's going to do something. He's not going to stand there all day.

Q: What do you find to be the most common fault that is made in schooling horses over ditches?

A: The biggest mistake that is made in schooling a horse over a ditch is this: The horse approaches the ditch. He stops a couple of times. He jumps it once. He stops a couple of times. Then he jumps it again, and then you say "Good Boy" and take him home. The next time out the same procedure is going to happen. He's going to stop a couple of times. You're going to say "Get going." He'll go. Then he's going to stop at the next ditch, and so on. This is why you've got to get it done all in one day.

Q: With this intensive schooling program, aren't you likely to get the horse in a complete lather and into a bit of a state?

A: It can happen. You do have to be a little hard on the horse. You do have to insist, but it saves a lot of fighting throughout the years if you do it all in one day. I find that in the long run it has always paid off to use this system.

Q: Do you use any sort of protective leg gear on the horse?

A: No. I'm not a great believer in things like that, unless the horse has got some particular fault. If, for example, he's a brusher, or overreaches, then I do use the appropriate boots, but otherwise I don't make any exception.

Q: Have you found that using a rail in front of the ditch, giving the horse a groundline, or a rail over the ditch to add a little height which he is familiar with, might make the ditch initially more inviting?

A: I find that this gives the horse something more to use as an excuse to stop, if he wants to stop. If a horse is dithering on the edge of a small ditch and can't make up his mind whether to go or not, all he's got to do is step across it. If you've got a rail slightly in front of it, or over it, he's got to jump and make the spread which can be even more frightening at first than just stepping across the ditch. So I just use ditches as they are.

Q: How many hours have you actually spent on the back of any one horse using this method of teaching a horse to jump ditches all in one day?

A: I started at five o'clock in the morning with the horse I mentioned, who was so frightened he wouldn't go within seven yards of a ditch in the beginning, and then it took us three-quarters of an hour to get over it. Once he was over, the next couple of ditches I took him to he tried stopping. He gradually got the idea, and stopping in front of each one took less time. Well, I missed my lunch because, after all, my horse was in front of a ditch. We went on and on over the countryside looking for ditches because we didn't have many nearby. At three thirty or four o'clock in the afternoon we called it a day. He was then jumping big ditches at a fast canter and pulling—he couldn't get at them fast enough. And now he enjoys ditches, he'll jump them any way, with rails, or just big open ditches, any type at all, and there isn't a horse to touch him for jumping ditches. In my experience I've never had any further difficulties with any horse using the all-in-one-day system.

Beth Perkins competing on the Olympic horse Furtive at Badminton. *(Photo by Clive Hiles.)*

Training With Lars Sederholm

By
BETH PERKINS

Several years ago, champion eventer Beth Perkins spent six months in England to further her Eventing and general equine education with Lars Sederholm. This article was adapted from her personal notes by USCTA NEWS *editor Fifi Coles.*

My father was most fortunate to be able to purchase the Australian horse, Furtive, just after the Olympics in Munich. The Australian team was unable to return home with their horses due to a lengthy quarantine. Furtive was then shipped over to Lars in October. A friend of ours from Vermont, Mrs. J. H. McKnight, loaned me her grey mare, Mills, on whom I had done some eventing in the States. With these two horses I started my training as a working pupil for six months with Lars Sederholm at Waterstock.

LARS' WATERSTOCK TRAINING CENTER

Waterstock Training Center is located about 20 miles north of Oxford and about 70 miles from London. The Training center monopolizes most of the small village of Waterstock. Because riding land is limited, it is necessary to transport the horses to either common or chalk hills nearby for conditioning. Most events are not more than two hours away.

Waterstock House itself is a beautiful, big, grey stone house with well-kept lawns and garden in front including a sand arena under huge old trees. The stables surround a stone courtyard with five more wooden stables behind it, fitted with large box stalls. There are usually forty horses stabled at the Center.

Lars Sederholm is well-known to most people involved in Three-Day Eventing the world over. He is Swedish by birth and received much of his earlier training in the Swedish Army. Later he took a position with the dressage rider, Mrs.

Gold. He subsequently became the manager of a riding school located at Mrs. Gold's stable. With a thorough ground schooling in dressage, he began eventing and competed successfully in the early sixties, when he became the Leading Rider in England. Shortly after that he set up the Training Center where he has turned out many excellent riders and horses. One of his students, Richard Walker, won Badminton at the age of eighteen on a little 15.2 hand horse named Pasha. Chris Collins and his sister, Anna Collins, both well-known competitors in England who competed here at Ledyard Farm International Event, keep several of their horses at Waterstock. Lars also instructed Princess Anne at one time. Several American riders also have trained with him, including Sally Lord Ike, Mason Phelps, Meg Plum, and Evy Thorndike.

EVENTING HERE AND THERE

Generally speaking, the whole atmosphere of eventing in the United States is different than in England. For one thing, it is much smaller and less formal. Everyone knows everyone else who competes, even those just starting to compete. It is taken for fun and it is an exciting and happy sport. Eventing in England means business. One has fun at home and between events. Points are very important, and placing well at an event is not just a singular success, but is part of qualifying for future events.

HORSE'S FRAME OF MIND AND PHYSICAL WELL-BEING

What I would like to do is to assemble the notes that I took while I was learning with Lars Sederholm. I feel my attitude towards horses has changed and I am more of a thinking rider now. Now to start as basically as I can, I'll take the horse and what frame of mind and physical state he should be in when aiming toward one's goal.

To start with, the way events are set up and also the type of countryside affect the horse's work cycle. Most horses aiming for the spring events, i.e. Badminton, are brought in from the rough to stay in the stable day and night in December. This is the beginning of their intensive training. Once these events are over, they are turned out completely day and night. This is done gradually, of course, in a process called "roughing off." This usually lasts for two months, then the horses are started up again in July in preparation for the late summer and fall events. They are roughed off again for two months once these are finished. So that is really the ideal cycle, but unfortunately it gets messed up occasionally as many horses have lameness or other troubles. One thing—horses can stay out even in winter as there is lush grass all year round in England.

Now once the horse is inside for awhile, it helps to get him concentrating more on humans than on other horses. The horse and rider really get a very close relationship as most of the day they are together. The horse relies on the rider for food, grooming, getting led out on a lead shank to munch a little grass, and for something to entertain his mind. Being in a stall all day is horribly boring for an animal whose whole being is based on movement. The horse's state of mind is affected very much by his physical well-being. He is kept as comfortable as possible with rugs (blankets) being taken off and put on endlessly, according to the weather.

Grooming is very important, especially when you are just starting them up. The grooming differs in England. Many hours are spent on a clean horse because they believe it helps build and tone the muscles. The horses enjoy it and it keeps them relaxed. They brush and brush and rub briskly with a cloth over the same place and the muscles ripple. The hooves are oiled daily and shoes checked, etc.

For food, hardly any horses get more than one section of hay morning and night. Their grain is changed often according to the work they are doing. Always on rest days and the night before, or if a horse is lame and out of work for awhile, they get a bran mash. The thin horses often get special food once or twice a week. This is mostly boiled oats or boiled barley, and linseed for special horses, also lots of carrots, molasses, honey and apples. They had three feedings at Lars'. In the morning they got about three quarts of crimped oats and one quart racehorse cubes (full of vitamins and minerals), the same for lunch and twice that for supper. Horses not doing as much work as mine got pony cubes (more fattening but less energy-producing). Most good event horses got Convital at supper which is full of everything you could ever want. Some people fed cod liver oil, or that seaweed stuff. They also liked Spectrum-4.

ANALYZING AND UNDERSTANDING

The attitude that people have towards their horses is definitely respect for a living thing. It is very important to know and think of your horse's personality and how to help it to learn the quickest. Furtive was very much respected and loved and made much of. This was best for him because (of course he deserved it) he grew to trust people and by doing that he could carry on with a clear head, not mixed up with fear. Mills, who was temperamental, was treated with a pat or affection when she needed it for schooling purposes, so that she would know when she was good. Mostly she got discipline though. She needed to think forward, but she is awfully lazy. That is her whole problem; all of her resistance resulted from simply not wanting to work. Going on the bit meant work. She is very strong minded and working with her takes real thinking, patience and control.

EMOTIONS

When working or schooling horses it is very important not to let your emotions get involved. Only on trail rides, or in the stable can you really let yourself become emotional. You can fool around and become really good friends, but even then you should use your head.

ALWAYS HAVE A PLAN

When working at home, it is necessary to be very careful to think out just what you are going to teach the horse, what exercises you are going to do and WHY. Be sure it is very clear in your mind before you try it on the horse.

In dressage for example, when Mills was going well just before Tidworth and we wanted to keep her in a good happy forward-thinking state, I would decide what exercises I was going to do. She was about the best she could be at this point. There was no purpose in trying to squeeze in any last minute schooling. What I would do was this. I would make her walk forward and then just get her into the canter on a loose rein, keeping her moving forward while giving her good pats on the neck. Then I would trot and canter again the same way, then walk. Then pick up the reins and take up the sitting trot (better for my seat) using half-halts. I worked on the circle and straight ahead as well as on two tracks. If she was then where I wanted her I would go through a few movements from the test and leave her. If not, we worked on lengthening and shortening work, half-passes, shoulder-ins, in order to make her work. Then she would start going on the bit, and in balance.

For schooling and conditioning also, it is important for the rider to have a definite plan or schedule in mind and have the various stages clearly thought out so that the horse will be at his peak at the right time. I have a bad memory so I must be careful to record everything. I write out where and what I am going to do two weeks at a time. I keep track of my actual time spent on the horse, my gallops and everything, so I know exactly where we are.

Now, not only have your plan, but another thing to remember is—never be lazy on your horse's back—ever. Don't ever let go and round your back for even a minute, or give into your horse in regard to discipline. Concentrate to your utmost capacity so that you will become a thinking rider. From this will come self-confidence, which is extremely important for a successful competitor.

All this should carry through when competing at events. Whether it be dressage, cross-country or stadium, be a thinking rider, and stick to the plan you have made for yourself. When riding your dressage test, go into the ring and show the judge that your horse is the best. Walk the cross-country course as many times as necessary so that you know exactly where and how you are going to jump each fence—then stick with this plan no matter what you hear from others.

Because your horse is suitably fit due to the conditioning schedule he should still have a little left at the finish of the cross-country. The rider should think every minute while in the saddle, ride every inch of the course, yet still finish much less tired than the horse. Actually the rider will usually be breathing harder after finishing a stadium round than when finishing the cross-country course.

DEVELOPING THE SEAT

Developing a good seat, Lars says, is one of the most important aspects in the training of the rider. So much of having a good seat is "feel" and feel is a difficult thing to convey. Now the seat is the base of all functions and the center of balance. If the seat is stable then it is easy to correct most any other problem. Actually my problem was my seat. I was tipped forward and the center of balance was on my hands and there was no way they could be independent until my seat became secure.

The rider should sit on his three seat bones, slightly forward, directly over his feet. The legs must be lightly in contact with the horse at all times, always there, ready to communicate. The back and shoulders should be straight (with the shoulders dropped) without tension or rigidity, with the thighs lying flat against the saddle, so that the inside of them is on the saddle. The knees and thighs are best when they are relaxed, not gripping.

My biggest problem was to relax the thighs and not grip with them, yet sit deeply. When posting, especially with short stirrups, there ought to be a little daylight between the knees and the saddle if the knee joint is relaxed. Many riders have been taught to grip with the knee but the problem there is that it's impossible to get the lower leg lying against the horse where it is needed.

The legs must be relaxed and flexible—not like a vise on the horse. However, Lars said that if a horse doesn't respond to the leg aid, it can be a great asset to really clobber him with a great kick if he needs it. I used to think that kicking a horse was absolutely taboo. Well, it is just a strong aid or punishment. Sometimes I had to kick Mills until I could hear it smack hard in order to get her to go forward. Forward was one of her problems. But there is one important thing to remember! If, after a kick, the horse suddenly shoots forward, don't give in to your natural reaction by taking back with the hands. Train yourself to give to him. Let the horse go forward, even into a gallop. Only then bring him back and reward him, so that he knows he was correct in going forward to the leg.

We used to work on the longe quite a bit, as it is a good exercise to help deepen the seat and spread the seat bones. Lars also had us do lots of transitions, extensions, strike-offs to trot and canter, which really made me use my seat. I had been really messed up with a lot of equitation riding in the States, so it took me five months of steady work to develop any sort of seat.

After my seat developed, it was easier to regulate the leg aids, and I then understood what "having the leg there" meant. Even though all the aids work independently they must all be coordinated. It was wonderful to realize that when I kept the horse together with my seat (the horse in balance), I could actually give away one rein (slide it forward and let it go loose), and the horse would stay in balance. I could give away both reins with the same result.

Lars used to have us use half-halts to bring

the horse really back and up, and then tell us to give, and ride him forward into the bit again. With a half-halt, I could feel the horse come back and up more, almost prancing in a way. Lars calls it "dancing" underneath you. But this is a fine-line sort of thing and takes a lot of "feel." In the same way, a horse should come into a halt (dancing into the halt) with all his legs underneath him. Half-halts should be practiced that way only at home. During a test just a closing of the hand on the outside rein should do. When the horse does become balanced and "dance," it is important to be soft with the hands and ride him forward into the bit again. Lars' motto is *"in balance, forward"* which if you think about it applies to everything, even life!

Generally speaking, there should be no tension in the rider's body, as that is resistance to the horse moving forward. Often I was amazed at Lars . . . to see how much he flowed with the horse, in absolute rhythm with it, although he did not have classic form. Now, one of my problems, for instance, was that I tended to go too much with the horse. He told me to practice being $\frac{1}{10}$th of a second behind the horse in jumping. This way I could be sure the horse was going out in front of me and my leg. If the horse is not in front of the rider, he will be a stopper. The reason horses hadn't stopped with me before, in spite of this, was because I compensated by keeping contact. Thank goodness I hadn't dropped them, or they would have stopped every time.

HANDS

Speaking of contact brings me to the subject of hands. Now, different types of horses and their problems take a different sort of hand. Often one type of hand will stop working all of a sudden, so never be afraid to change it. For instance, with a horse that fusses and jerks his head up, a low fixed hand on the withers is a very steadying position. With this fixed hand the horse soon realizes that he is punishing himself when he fusses with his head. You can also be much softer with the hand in this position. When the hands are up you can't help much, unless you've learned how to be soft without always taking on them. However, a higher hand is useful when the horse tends to rush, or is on the forehand in jumping. Then it is important to look for moments when the horse is light so that the rider can be light in return.

A good exercise with a "rusher" is to pick up and drop the contact. This way the horse doesn't always have the hand to lean on and fight against. They soon learn to listen and carry themselves.

With a horse that gets overbent, or on the forehand, it is helpful to make a very quick upwards motion (not back) with the hands, then right back to the normal position.

All in all, the reins should not be too short or too long. Don't be afraid to change the position on the reins, as this often helps to get a new feel of the horse's mouth. But no matter what, be sure to have a sufficient enough hold so that the reins don't slip through the hands, thus avoiding having to shorten them all the time.

Now to get a horse to relax in the jaw, you will often have to play with the mouth. This does not mean sawing back and forth so that his head is going from side to side (which you see with riders sometimes). It does mean light and varied vibrations when needed. This is truly an art, because it involves "feel" which comes through experience. Think, when you are working on the mouth, that you are working on the jaw, and not the whole neck. When the jaw is soft, the horse will flex his neck. Those "perfect" still hands that one often sees are usually unsympathetic hands, always slightly pulling on the mouth. This used to be one of my problems.

One important thing to remember, I found is—with the hands, or anything—be definite. Make your aids good and clear. This will avoid much confusion to the horse, making the training process much easier.

THE HORSE

Conditioning

The conditioning program starts from the moment we bring the horses in from the rough. First, we trim them up, pull the tail and mane and spend a lot of time grooming to tone up the muscles. If it's the winter (as in England you can ride all year long), a good clipping helps a lot. Sweating too much will impede conditioning, and will cause a fit horse to lose condition. Also, with a clipped horse you can watch the development of the neck muscles, those along the top of the rump, and those at the back of the hindquarters.

Feeding

In a conditioning program, the feeding of the horse is very important. I noticed that the "Badminton horses" always seemed to be in good flesh at peak condition. This wasn't so with Little Secret, the horse that I did so much eventing with in the States. He was always skin and bones. At Lars' we kept the feed up, increasing the amount of oats in their feed as soon as the horses started to settle down.

However, they were not allowed to get too heavy as carrying those extra pounds is hard on them. When Furtive, who is an older horse, started getting heavier, Lars said, "Don't get him too heavy, as it's like a boxer who in later years puts on weight. It's bound to affect him."

Tar Roads

The horses were started by walking them on tar roads for the first three weeks. Most of the working was done "on the bit," asking them to really walk out. The hard road helps toughen up the legs. The English always do a good deal of trotting, too, on hard roads. We had no fields nearby, so we trucked about three miles to find rolling hills where we did our conditioning trots and gallops.

"Loose Canters"

We worked at "loose canters" two to three times a week. The purpose of this is to allow the horse to learn to balance himself without having any hands to rely on. It helps to gain fitness while relaxing the horse. The first loose canter was three minutes, the next time six, then eight minutes, which was repeated several times before increasing the canters, subsequently by two minutes more, depending upon the fitness of each horse and how much other work they did that day.

Three Times a Day

Usually we rode each horse three times daily! The work was varied—schooling, a hack, a loose canter or later jumping; an early morning gallop (with a few hours to recuperate) and then a hack. We never worked a long time on any one thing, but when we worked we put the horse on the bit, as Lars believes that that is the only way that they fully use themselves. Another thing that Lars felt very strongly about was to make a point of patting the horse (quite a bit) when it is going well on the bit, or doing whatever you asked it to do. It helps the rider relax as well as the horse. It is very pleasing to the horse, as well as an excellent training aid—rewarding the horse for doing well, particularly when it may have been punished, and then goes correctly.

When we hacked, the horses were allowed to enjoy themselves more, but they were still made to go on contact and use themselves. The hacking time during the early stages of conditioning remained the same, but the trots were gradually increased. Later the hacks were longer until they reached 2½ hours. At this point the horses were quite fit and most of the time was spent trotting. It was important to be aware if the horse became the slightest bit tired at any time during the conditioning. If this happened it was time to call it quits for the day.

Fast Work

A few weeks before the horse's first event we started our fast work. Early morning is a great time for it. We started with slow gallops around a field interspersed with trots and walks. When

Mills and Beth Perkins winning the Advanced division at the Dunham Three-Day Event, Quebec, Canada in 1973. *(Photo by Alix Coleman.)*

galloping, Lars recommends a good short contact, while trying for a steady and stable feeling with the upper body. We mostly galloped and trotted in pairs or groups of four. The horses were actually kept stirrup to stirrup, unless one was a kicker. Then they still galloped abreast but farther apart. This teaches young horses how to gallop correctly, developing their stride and rhythm. It also makes passive horses more competitive, while helping all horses to keep going. A good galloping horse will really reach out in front, with the hindquarters well underneath. If you should have a puller and there is quite a distance to go, a bridged rein will save your arms. Although you can't slow them or stop them with it, you can maintain pace.

Well, we continued to increase the length of the gallops, until, before Tidworth, we galloped every other day—two miles at a steady cross-country pace, then one mile at a good clip (steeplechase speed) with a real burst at the end (pipe-opener) for a few hundred yards. Sometimes we only did one mile of steady galloping and one mile fast work towards the end. This was all done in a soft flat field.

Hill Work

Before Badminton, the horses (who were now quite fit) were trucked to some steep chalk hills. The hills went nearly straight up. Giving the horses their heads, we trotted to the top, riding out of the saddle and clutching the mane. Walking at the top a bit to let them catch their breath, we then did the same thing over again. Well, there was another hill that went up gradually from the bottom; near the top it had a very steep bank, and then straight up a short distance. We did this one at a slow gallop all the way, leaping the bank and on up the rest of the hill. We finished up with just one more trotting hill.

When Furtive was able to do this, he was fit and ready to compete at Badminton.

How to Build a Cross-Country Course

By
ROGER HALLER

A special bonus for builders, these skilled observations on the design of a cross-country course also provide interesting insights into the cross-country phase itself.

FENCE DESIGN

There are seven basic types of obstacles which should be on every course: 1) straightforward uprights and spreads; 2) ditches, either open or in conjunction with a fence; 3) banks; 4) drops; 5) water, to be jumped over, into or out of; 6) brush, often called bullfinches; and 7) multiple obstacles. Each type will vary according to the intended level of difficulty.

At the Training level the *straightforward fences*, for example, should be built to maximum specifications and made to be galloped at boldly. At the Preliminary level, however, the approach may be a little more complicated, for the rider is beginning to be asked to choose one of a number of lines. The rider's approach to these fences becomes even more important at the Intermediate and Advanced levels, where his control and the horse's responsiveness are tested by the need to ride a certain line.

Ditches at the Training level should occur in front of or behind a fence, preferably behind. A horse should be able to get into (and out of) an open ditch if it occurs at this level; otherwise an open ditch could be a bit much on a Training course. An open ditch makes a good obstacle on a Preliminary course, however. Intermediate and Advanced courses should offer increasingly large and wide ditch obstacles. For example, a very large ditch before a very large upright would be good on an Advanced course.

A rider wants to develop his horse's boldness and confidence over water, and *water obstacles* on a cross-country course should help him do this. Therefore, they should be introduced carefully, if at all, at the Training level, remembering that the horse is to be encouraged, not discouraged. At the Pre-Training and Training levels, crossing through unflagged water is a good preparation for a water obstacle. At the Training level this obstacle could be a small bank, to be jumped either into or out of water. Footing, of course, is of the utmost importance at all levels of competition.

At the Preliminary level, water may be combined with a fence. The obstacle should still be as straightforward as possible, however, so the horse can be bold and not get into trouble; this is of the utmost importance. Make sure the water is absolutely safe! On an Intermediate course water may appear as part of a combination; the rider must decide how he wants to get into it. Then, at the Advanced level, turns, combinations, and stride problems may be incorporated.

Brush and *Bullfinches* are almost the same at every level. The major difference is the amount of daylight evident, for these fences get thicker and wider as the levels advance, testing the horse's confidence and trust.

Banks and *Drops* should be straightforward and relatively small at the Training level. At the Preliminary level these obstacles should be built up to maximum, but they should still be relatively straightforward. A good Intermediate version could call for a maximum jumping effort by virtue of increased size or perhaps by a fence on top of a bank (a Normandy bank). Distance problems can become a factor at the Advanced level.

Multiple obstacles, combining these types of fences, are the meat of a cross-country course and are unique to the sport of Combined Training. At the Training level they should be very straightforward—steps would be a good example. An "L" is inappropriate at the Training level unless its legs are very long. A Preliminary course may present a series of banks, ditches, or drops. Alternate lines through the combination may be presented at this level because the horse should be responding to the rider. For example, the competitor may encounter short-legged "L's" with a corner option, or "V's" where he has to choose his line. But no spread of complicated fences or ditches should be presented at the Preliminary level; the horse is always to be encouraged to jump boldly.

At the Intermediate and Advanced levels, multiple obstacles take on a different character. Intermediate will incorporate changes in terrain, require a big line and a big effort. A coffin is a typical example; this type of obstacle is difficult but straightforward. At the Advanced level, multiple obstacles can get very technical, requiring many rider decisions and a very responsive horse. A series of fences downhill involving turns will do this. Multiple obstacles like this are very difficult, but still relatively safe.

COURSE DESIGN

Any organizer faces some limitations from the very beginning. He or she needs a certain amount of acreage, and the amount available for a cross-country course will probably be limited by the fact that only a few areas will be suitable for dressage, stadium and parking. After setting aside these areas, the course builder will walk over the remaining terrain, picking out possible spots for fences, and trying to put in as many of the seven types as possible. He or she will also consider what kind of course is to be built: Preliminary, Training, or the like.

When planning the course, the designer should keep the following rules of thumb in mind:

—The golden rule is that the most difficult fences should be in the middle third of the course. The first third should prepare the horse and rider for the most demanding fences, while the final obstacles—especially at a Three-Day Event, where the horses have gone a distance—should not be too demanding. They may be large and require a large jumping effort, but should be honest and straightforward. This does not mean there should be great variety in the level of difficulty of the fences. On the whole, the fences should be even and uniform in difficulty.

—If the course must cross its own line at some point, it should do so in an open field with good visibility and not near a fence.

—Fences should look appropriate to the terrain.

—Consider the time of the year the event will be held, and how this will affect the course. Footing and depth of water are especially apt to change.

—Also keep the sun in mind when planning a course; don't head riders into the sun in the afternoon. The time of year will make a difference here, too.

—Avoid obligatory flags; they are hard for competitors to remember. Put a fence at that point of the course instead.

—It is better to have fewer fences, nicely built and with much variety, than a number of fences without variety put in just for length's sake; remember, you can always add to the course in successive years.

—The face of obstacles should be at least twenty feet wide, although they may occasionally be narrower if the designer wishes to test control. This is true even of Pre-training, where a wide face can encourage galloping on.

—When the competitor will be jumping from light into dark, make the fence relatively small. It should be large, in order to be seen well, when the direction is from dark to light.

—Always check the proposed course by mapping it out; it should flow smoothly and encourage galloping on boldly.

—It is better to build up a fence by using imposing materials than to try to make it impressive by dressing it up or "decorating" it.

The course designer should also keep the recent rule changes in mind:

—The number of lettered combinations is now limited to one for every ten obstacles.

—The number of drop fences has been limited to two on a course, and the extent of the drop is now regulated according to level.

—Water may not be more than 1′-8″ deep at the point of landing and for five meters beyond.

CONSTRUCTION OF OBSTACLES

In general, the golden rule for fence building is "the bigger and solider, the better." The fence will be better jumped, longer lasting, and unlikely to delay the time schedule by needing repair. Therefore, *use big, solid timber.* This is especially true at the Pre-training and Training levels where horses are apt to get careless. If the course builders have to stretch their budget, they should buy big rails (8″ to 10″ in diameter) and split them into half-rounds.

The second general principle is to *try to get a nice variety of material* for the fences. For example, pine, cedar—each with bark and without—white birch and other naturally varying material add to the attractiveness of the courses.

Third, the fence builders should always try to *build as safely as possible.* For example, banks should be put in several months before the event, so the dirt has time to settle and good footing is assured.

One suggestion for improving the safety of a fence is to have the top rail roped on, so it can be cut if a horse gets hung up. If this is done, however, it is essential to have a brace at an angle (see illustration A). The combination of an angled brace and a relatively small nail could be used instead of a rope. When using either of these methods, it is important to remember that the top element of an obstacle should not be the furthest forward—all rails should be on the same line, if the fence is a vertical, or, if possible, the top rail should be set into the post.

The best way to join panels is to get a big post and notch it (see illustration B). Post holes should be a minimum of twenty inches deep; two feet is better, and soft ground may

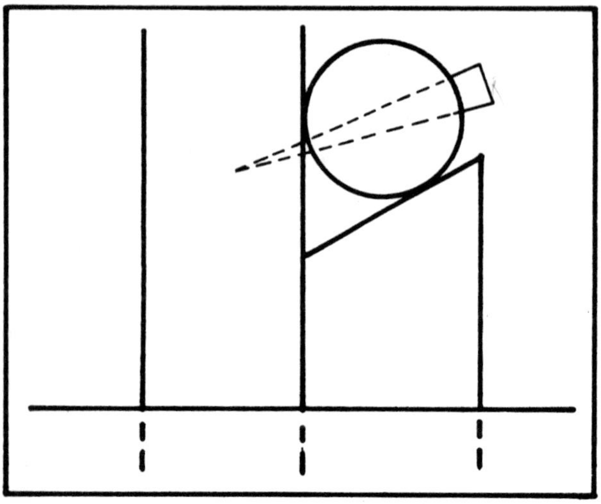

Illustration A

call for more. Like banks, the posts should be put in as easily as possible, to allow the dirt around them to set.

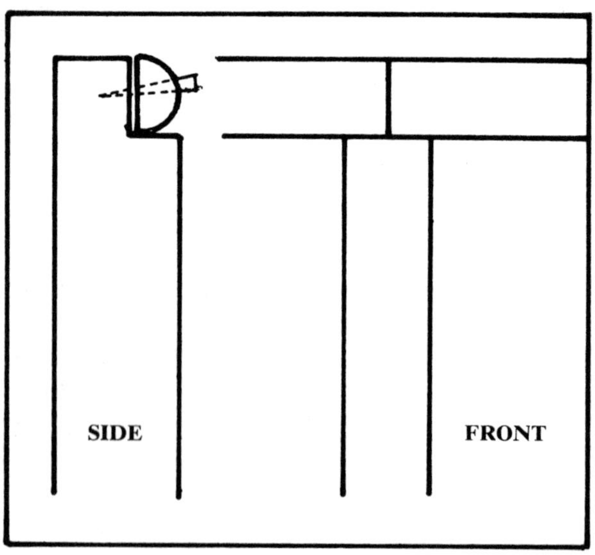

Illustration B

Rails may be attached to posts by bolts, ropes, nails, or wire. Carriage bolts, available in most hardware stores, are good for post-and-rail, but expensive; for telephone poles and railroad ties, anchor bolts or two-foot nails are required. Both can be gotten from construction supply companies and some hardware stores. If wire is used, it should be at least 8 gauge; 11 gauge is preferred, and 16 gauge is necessary for revetment.

To revet a bank, stack railroad ties or similar material vertically between the bank and posts imbedded in the ground at the base of the bank. Reinforce the supporting posts by wiring them to stakes driven into the bank near the top, and then fill in the area between the railroad ties and the bank, covering the bracing stakes in the process (see illustration C). When revetting a ditch, don't square it at the bottom. Put one or two railroad ties near the top, if necessary, and then lay a telephone pole before the ditch to provide a take-off point and prevent digging up of the revetment (see illustration C).

FLAGGING AND NUMBERING THE COURSE

It is important to make numbers, flags, and directional markers out of good material—if properly taken care of such signs are the least expensive in the long run and they add a lot to the course's attractiveness. Quarter-inch exterior plywood and good paint are recommended. Several people report that plastic shatters and masonite or pressed board doesn't last. The DVCTA reported it had had good success with pegboard, since the holes allowed workers to nail up and take down signs without damaging them. Plywood should have nail holes drilled, not hammered, in; furthermore, the nails should not be hammered all the way in when attaching signs, so they can be taken down easily. Markers and numbers should not be left out all year. Attention to small details such as these adds the finishing touches to a well-built course.

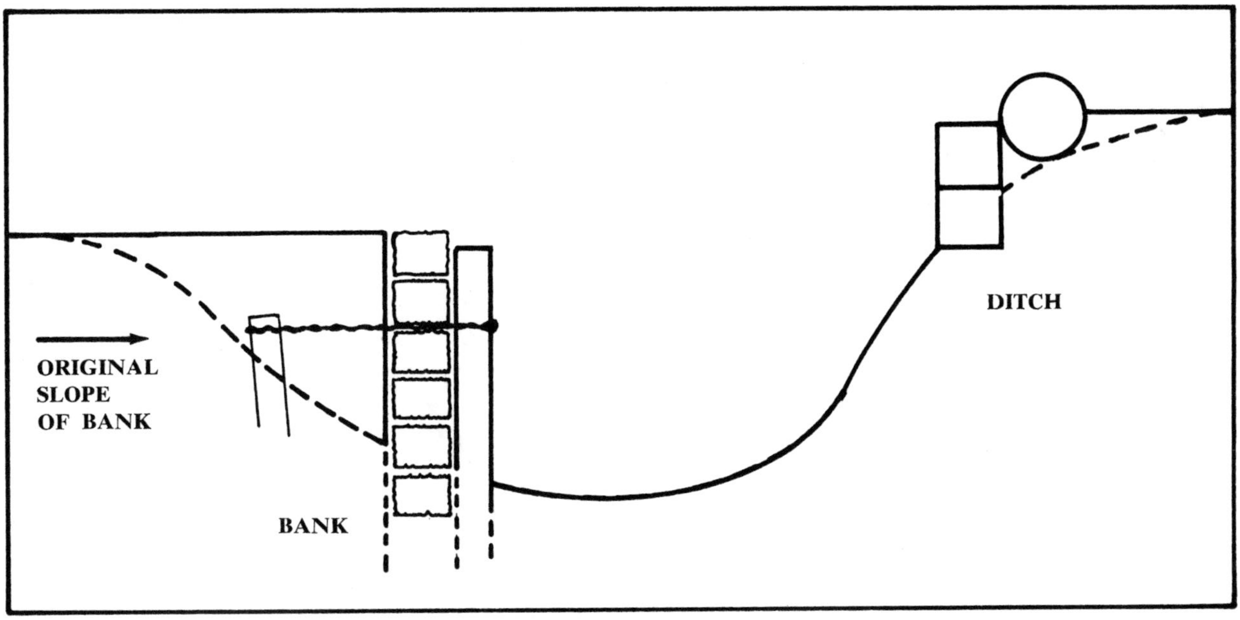

Illustration C

ABOUT THE AUTHORS

HARLAN ABBEY
is a journalist and the author of *Showing Your Horse*. He is thoroughly conversant with the horse show scene, having served alternately as exhibitor, announcer, steward, and judge.

RICHARD B. BARSALEAU, D.V.M.
is a member of the Endurance Committee of the California State Horsemen's Association and is a former chairman of the Judge's Committee, American Association of Equine Practitioners.

JEREMY BEALE
is a British Army Major who has competed at all of the major European Three-Day Events. He is now director of Fox Hollow Farms Equestrian Center in Chester Springs, Pennsylvania, where he schools riders and their horses for combined training competition.

MARIAN BOND
is a professional writer and photojournalist who lives in Los Angeles with her executive husband, three children, and a variety of horses, dogs, and cats. She began writing about horses when her children started riding and has since become a regular contributor to the top riding magazines.

FIFI COLES
is Editor of the *USCTA News* and an active competitor on the event circuit. Her best known horse was Sparrow Hawk, whom she rode to fourth place as Leading Horse of the Year in the U.S. in 1971.

E. HARTLEY EDWARDS
is one of the best-known names in the English riding world. The editor of *Riding* Magazine, he is also head of a firm of saddlers and his book *Saddlery* is a classic in its field. With all his duties, he still finds time to lecture to riding clubs throughout Britain.

E. RUSSELL GOODALE
started riding in Venezuela, schooled at the Virginia Combined Training Center, and went on to many victories with his horse Dominion Cloudburst. A contributor to riding magazines, he has also been Secretary of the Rockridge Hunt.

MARSHALL GRAY
is Assistant Coach and Stable Manager for the United States Three-Day Team under Coach Jack LeGoff. An outstanding horsewoman in her own right, she has a vast background in the equestrian world.

ROGER HALLER
is Vice President of the USCTA, Chairman of its Area II, and Director of the Essex Horse Trials in New Jersey. A rider as well, he competed on the outstanding event horse Golden Griffin for five years before it was donated to the Three-Day Team.

SHEILA WALL HUNDT
is Chairman of the Radnor Hunt-Hahnemann Horse Trials Committee and an honorary Whipper-In of Hounds in Malvern, Pennsylvania. She has been an editor of *The Saturday Evening Post* and *TV Guide*, and is the author of *Horseback Riding* and *A Beginner's Guide to Horseback Riding*.

JACK LeGOFF
is the Three-Day Coach of the United States Equestrian Team.

CATHERINE McWILLIAMS
is a Californian who now teaches and trains horses at Bear Ridge Riding Club in Pleasantville, New York. She is currently working on a book about dressage and her prize-winning Thoroughbred, The Shadow, is working on his Fourth Level dressage test.

PATTY MONTALI
has taught art and riding at a private school in Maryland, in addition to schooling horses and competing in combined training and dressage events. Her column, "Answers From Patty," was a monthly feature of *Horse Play* Magazine.

DIANE L. MORGAN
has been a Steward of the American Horse Shows Association since 1960 and also owns and operates Cedar Creek Stables, Inc., in Fort Wayne, Indiana.

GEORGE MORRIS
is one of America's foremost instructor/riders. A former member of the USET, he has coached countless finalists and winners of the Medal and Maclay Awards, both of which he won himself at age 14.

SALLY O'CONNOR
has been a Governor of the USCTA for three years and is a member of the AHSA Combined Events Committee. Born in England, she was one of the founders of the United States Dressage Federation and is an AHSA dressage judge as well as a contributor to many riding magazines.

BETH PERKINS
was raised on a horse farm in Vermont where all of her family participate in Horse Trials and breed horses for eventing and hunting. At 19, she was a member of the Three-Day Team that won the 1974 World Championships at Burghley.

SHARON SAARE
is Director of Distance Riding for the Appaloosa Horse Club, Inc., a member and judge of the North American Trail Ride Conference, and a leading figure in the world of long-distance riding. Her books include *Endurance Riding And Management, Know All About Trail Riding,* and the *Appaloosa Horse Club Distance Riding Manual.*

MARY ANN SEBREY
is a newspaper writer and photographer whose love of horses has made her a frequent contributor to riding magazines.

ROBIN SERFASS
is a native Californian who has ridden since the age of ten. She is Assistant Editor of *Horses* and will soon graduate from UCLA, having left college several times in the past to concentrate on riding and showing.

GINA M. STATON
is a freelance writer who specializes in horses and is also active in teaching, training, and showing. She lives in Florida, where her veterinarian husband has an exclusively equine practice.

HEATHER SMITH THOMAS
is a top magazine writer and the author of three books: *A Horse in Your Life, Your Horse And You,* and *Horses: Their Breeding, Care and Training.* With her husband and two children, she runs a cattle ranch in Salmon, Idaho and breeds her own horses which she rides in long distance competition.

BILL THROGMORTON, D.V.M.
is an approved NATRC judge and an approved endurance ride veterinarian in the American Association of Equine Practitioners. He is the author of the NATRC *Judge's Manual* and a contributor to the AAEP *Guide for Endurance and Competitive Judges.*

CHUCK TYLER
spent 20 years in the Marine Corps where he worked on *Leatherneck* Magazine, and served as a combat photographer in Korea and photo officer in Vietnam. He has been on the editorial staff of both *Horse & Rider* and *Horse and Horseman,* and is now in the desert recreation business.

ANN DAVIS WILLIAMS
has been riding and showing horses for most of her life. The winner of many trophies and ribbons throughout the intermountain region, she has been Associate Editor of *The Utah Equestrian* and writes frequently on horses and horsemanship.

JIMMY WOFFORD
represented the United States in both the Mexico and Munich Olympics, as well as in the 1967 Pan American Games and the World Championships after Mexico. Eventing since childhood, he is the product of a family whose lives are devoted to international competition.